DUDLEY WRIGHT:
WRITER, TRUTHSEEKER & FREEMASON

DUDLEY WRIGHT

Writer,
Truthseeker
& Freemason

JOHN BELTON

Westphalia Press
An Imprint of the Policy Studies Organization
Washington, DC
2016

Dudley Wright: Writer, Truthseeker & Freemason
All Rights Reserved © 2016 by Policy Studies Organization

Westphalia Press
An imprint of Policy Studies Organization
1527 New Hampshire Ave., NW
Washington, D.C. 20036
info@ipsonet.org

ISBN-10: 1-63391-336-8
ISBN-13: 978-1-63391-336-3

Cover and interior design by Jeffrey Barnes
jbarnesbook.design

Daniel Gutierrez-Sandoval, Executive Director
PSO and Westphalia Press

Updated material and comments on this edition
can be found at the Westphalia Press website:
www.westphaliapress.org

Contents

Preface...vii

Dudley Wright:
Writer, Truthseeker & Freemason............................1

Bibliography...49

Disambiguation...79

Appendix I:
Excerpt from *The Masonic Secretaries' Journal*.......81

Appendix II
Excerpt from *The Islamic Review*...............................85

Preface

Though little known outside of Masonic circles, or perhaps even within them, Dudley Wright was a prolific author. As he wandered the highways and byways of religion, he published approximately 30 books and 200 short essays on various esoteric, spiritual, and religious subjects in a variety of Masonic, Buddhist, Islamic, Jewish, Christian, and theosophical magazines, and hundreds of short reports in his capacity as the Masonic Editor of The Times newspaper of London.

I first discovered Dudley Wright through his revision of Gould's History of Freemasonry published in 1931 in Britain and in a further revision in 1936 in the United States, but it was the discovery of his other publications that really ignited my interest. Many of us, as we grow into maturity, ask ourselves questions about the meaning of "life and everything" and so did Wright. But in his case, he wrote done those journeys and published them.

Wright was quite reticent regarding his own life, he had entries in Who's Who but the detail proved somewhat elusive. To make contact with John Tomalin, by chance a Freemason, and more importantly a distant relative of Dudley Wright, who untangled his early life as a Last rather than a Wright, goes a special note of gratitude. However, his biographical contribution to the Masonic Secretaries' Journal of 1919, is reproduced here (courtesy of the Library and Museum of Freemasonry in London) provides the only personally written insight – and the only photographic image found.

That his life should be published in the United States is a special surprise, for Wright himself never traveled there, and his contacts and friendship were developed by good old-fashioned mails written on paper and crossing the Atlantic by ship. Wright and Joseph Fort Newton (author of The Builders) developed a special friendship, and while both of them were Freemasons, they were drawn together by shared social and religious attitudes. Wright wrote for American masonic magazines The Builder and subsequently for The Master Mason.

Wright went through a vast gamut of religions, settling upon Islam and was a part of the moderate Ahmadiyya sect for two parts of his life. But even in his earliest writing days in 1907 for the Christian Commonwealth some trends were to the fore. This journal was devoted to the "Christian Unity Movement" which persistently attacked the evils of sectarianism and denominationalism. So already there was a close approach to the values and ethos of Newton's Universalist Church, and indeed Newton's sermons were published there.

While the contact between Wright and Newton clearly predates 1916 and flowered when they both became involved in The Builder, that legendary masonic magazine run out of Iowa. It collected a small group of enthusiastic masonic wordsmiths who drifted away after the change of the publisher in 1924 to write elsewhere. The prior decade saw a flowering of masonic journalism that remains unique. It was the disapproval of that diversity of Masonic thought by the Masonic powers which caused other groups to rise up and take the place of The Builder after its demise. This part of the Masonic history of the United States has not been well studied, so perhaps this study will prompt more investigation.

The chance to catalog the breadth of Wright's prodigious writing activities has been taken by the inclusion of the most complete bibliography it has been possible to construct. Wright did tend to use material several times, sometimes serializing what would later become a book, and this record will enable the reader to see how Wright operated as a wordsmith writing for a living. In doing so, he left behind a paper trail that has been followed assiduously. It is likely that his articles were also published in various masonic magazines throughout the British Empire and maybe elsewhere in the United States as well; one has to stop somewhere in the chase.

As this work progressed, the interest of various people in Wright came to light, and I acknowledge their help and enthusiasm. Paul Rich had a couple of articles published in the Philalethes magazine, Simon Mayers had looked at his religious affiliations and assisted in the religious aspects of the work on Wright, and he would wish me to thank the Sisters at the Sion Centre for Dialogue and Encounter in London for their kindly assistance to him. The staff at the Library and Museum of Freemasonry in London was interested because of his editorial work on the long running English masonic weekly The Freemason. My thanks go to Larissa Watkins and the Library of the House of the Temple, in Washington DC, for scanning materials and to Brent Morris and the Scottish Rite Research Society for the permission to reuse material published in Heredom. But especially my thanks go to Paul Rich for his interest in Dudley Wright and his suggestion that it be published with extra materials, especially the bibliography.

It only remains to hope that the reader gets as much pleasure from reading as was got in the researching, and perhaps that further study of the difficulties faced by masonic writers in the United States which indirectly led to the formation of the North Carolina Lodge of Research and the Philalethes Society.

DUDLEY WRIGHT:
Writer, Truthseeker & Freemason

Brother Dudley Wright, a dear gracious, brotherly man, who reminds me of Dr. Johnson and knows more about things old, odd, and interesting than any man has a right to know. He is a perpetual delight, as much for his loyal good-will as for his wide learning, and his friendship is sweet.

— Joseph Fort Newton, "British Freemasonry" (1924)

We are Truthseekers; we seek the Truth because we know that that Truth will make us free. As Truth-seekers we must keep an open mind to receive it from whatever source it may come.

— Dudley Wright, Spiritualism *(1912)*

Dudley Wright (1868–1949) was a prolific author who wrote on an eclectic range of subjects. In addition to his works on Free-masonry, he also published many articles and books on various religious traditions, including Judaism, Christianity (and in particular Catholicism), Islam, Buddhism, Druidism, and various mystical traditions. In addition to religion and spiritualism, he also had an early keen interest in psychic phenomena, the occult, and the preternatural. Wright considered himself a "Truthseeker." As he explained in *The Masonic Secretaries' Journal* in 1919, his principal goal was to "trace the unvarying basis from the philosophic standpoint of all religious systems."[1] Though the form of this goal changed over time, it permeated his discourse from 1906 until 1919, and laid the foundation for much of his future studies until his death in 1949. Wright published approximately thirty books and booklets, and more than 200 articles and essays in a wide variety of Masonic, Buddhist, Islamic, Jew-

---

1 Anon, "Our Contributors," *The Masonic Secretaries' Journal,* 2:6 (January 1919), 328–29. He stated that this was "an Islamic belief."

ish, Catholic, Theosophical, and other religious periodicals. According to a recent study by Dr. Paul Calderwood, Wright also published about 815 short articles relating to Freemasonry in *The Times* newspaper from 1919 until 1933.[2] During this period he was the Masonic Editor of *The Times*.

Whilst his articles and books reveal a broad spiritual journey, and a search for the "truth" and the underlying foundations of all myths and religions, what little is known about his personal life reveals a somewhat enigmatic figure. From his entry in *Who's Who*, and a biographical entry in the *Masonic Secretaries' Journal*, we know that he was born in Cheyne Walk, Chelsea, on 19 February 1868. According to the biographical entry in the *Masonic Secretaries' Journal*, he was previously employed by "the ill fated *Standard* newspaper." The entry also notes that "his acquaintance with Pitman's system of shorthand dates back to the year 1878"—i.e. by the age of ten![3]

Very little else is known for certain about Wright's personal life. However, whilst working on this article, Bro. John Tomalin of Albert Lodge No. 4320, whose genealogical research uncovered a personal family connection to Dudley Wright, reached out. According to Tomalin, Dudley Wright was born Frederick William James Last, on 19 February 1868, in Chelsea. Whilst it is impossible to verify this with absolute certainty, the 1901 census records and other documents for Frederick Last do correlate extremely closely to the biographical information found for Dudley Wright (e.g. the exact same date and city of birth, and both registered as having a son named Guy Alexander born in 1901).

The 1901 census record for Frederick Last has him as living with his first wife and family in Littlehampton on Sea, where he was employed as an engineer's clerk. We know that Wright was living in Harrow-on the Hill at the time of the 1911 census with his second wife and three children, one of whom was from his previous marriage. Not one to live life by halves, his life included three marriages (Elizabeth Thompson, Ann Elizabeth Knappet, and Elizabeth Florence Maria Wright). According to his (self-) entry in the *Who's Who* (from 1911 onwards), he was educated at Ware and at King's and University Colleges in London, but the precise details of his education have proven elusive. Dudley Wright died on 7 March 1949 at St Andrews Hospital, Bow, London. There is a short obituary for Dudley Wright in the *Freemasons*

---

2 Paul Calderwood, *Freemasonry and the Press in the Twentieth Century* (Farnham, Surrey: Ashgate, 2013), appendix 4. *The Times* was then the leading broadsheet paper.

3 "Our Contributors," *The Masonic Secretaries' Journal,* 2:6 (January 1919), 328.

The only known likeness of Dudley Wright.
Source: *The Masonic Sectretaries' Journal, 1919.*

Chronicle of 9 April 1949, which observed that "the death has taken place, in a London Hospital, of Bro. Dudley Wright, who may be remembered by the older generation, as a once prominent writer on Masonic subjects."

SEARCHING FOR THE FOUNDATION OF RELIGIOUS SYSTEMS (1906–1920)

It is perhaps part of the nature of human curiosity to examine belief systems as a source of personal spiritual enlightenment. Wright engaged actively in this pursuit for most of his life, but what makes him unusual is that he leaves a trail of this search in his writings. His keen dislike of dogma led him to seek the "true religion." In his examination of the shared foundations of Buddhism, Islam, the Hebrew and Christian scriptures, the occult and psychical science, Wright frequently hinted at an unnamed pre-existing religion which provided the unsullied "original pure foundation" to all religions (i.e. a sort of universal Ur-religion). His quest for the underlying truth and shared foundation of all religious systems, which brought him to Buddhism in 1912 and Islam in 1915, also brought him, probably via his interest in Theosophy and his interest in the Temple of Solomon and the ancient myths and legends of various religions, to Freemasonry (perhaps, as it is stated in Anderson's 1723 *Constitutions,* as "that religion upon which all men can agree"). This search resonated with the approach of Bro. Rev. Joseph Fort Newton and must have been a real bond of friendship.

Whilst it is likely that Dudley Wright had already begun his search for "the truth" some years earlier, it was in 1906, at the age of thirty-eight, with the publication of a booklet entitled *The Fourth Dimension,* that he started to share his ideas and conclusions with the world. According to his autobiographical entry in *The Masonic Secretaries' Journal* of 1919, this was his first published work, and it was "sold out within three months of publication."[4] In 1908, Wright published a series of short essays and translations relating to the Hebrew and Christian scriptures in periodicals such as *Spiritual Power,* the *Homiletic Review* and the *Bible Review.* Wright also published his first book, *Was Jesus an Essene?,* in this year. In this book, Wright argued that Jesus was a member of the Essenes—a Jewish sect at the end of the Second Temple period[5]—rather than a divine being and a part of the

---

4 "Our Contributors," *The Masonic Secretaries' Journal,* 2:6 (January 1919), 328–29.

5 The Essenes were a Jewish religious sect, distinct from the Pharisees and Sadducees, that flourished in the final centuries of the Second Temple. Very little is known about them.

Trinity.[6] At this stage of his life, and until he converted to Catholicism in the early 1930s, Wright did not consider himself a Christian. When he wrote a letter to the *Jewish Chronicle* in 1910, he explicitly identified himself as "a Gentile, though not a Christian reader of the Jewish Chronicle."[7]

Whilst he held Jesus in high esteem, he was often critical of "orthodox" forms of Christianity. *Was Jesus an Essene?* contains the earliest evidence of this antipathy. Wright argued that it is probable that Jesus and the Essenes were influenced by Eastern religions including Parseeism and Buddhism, and that Jesus spent some time in monasteries in India and Tibet. According to Wright, the Catholic Church found this idea so inimical, it tried to bury the evidence in support of it. This reveals Wright's early stance towards what he referred to as "orthodox Christianity," which he concluded has "failed to catch any of the spirit of the teaching of Jesus."[8]

In addition to his conjectures about the origins of Jesus, Wright was also involved in speculations of a more occult and psychical nature. In 1908, he monitored a series of tests involving "thought-readers" for the *Annals of Psychical Science*.[9] He was the assistant editor of this periodical from January 1909, and the editor from October 1909 to September 1910. According to Wright, the purpose of this periodical was to report "serious and well-attested observations relative to the various psychical phenomena known and studied under the terms Telepathy, Clairvoyance ... Premonition, and objective Apparitions."[10] This "psychical science" approach to the study of spiritual truth was a reoccurring aspect of Wright's early discourse. In 1910, Wright published a booklet entitled *Spiritualism in Relation to the Doctrine of Immortality* and an article entitled "Can Reincarnation be Demonstrated?" These examined questions relating to reincarnation, immortality, and the fate of the soul. Wright argued that a non-dogmatic scientific approach to such investigations was essential. He was sceptical at this stage of his life not only about Christianity, but also about all the major religions, which he believed were built upon shared foundations, but had been buried beneath

6 Dudley Wright, *Was Jesus an Essene?* (Wimbledon: Power-Book, 1908), 7–57.

7 Letter from Dudley Wright to the Editor, *Jewish Chronicle*, 3 June 1910, 14.

8 Wright, *Was Jesus an Essene?*, 11–14, 17–18.

9 Dudley Wright, "More Professional 'Thought-Readers,'" *Annals of Psychical Science* 7:47 (November 1908), 532–33.

10 Dudley Wright, "The Annals of Psychical Science," in Dudley Wright, *Spiritualism in Relation to the Doctrine of Immortality* (Manchester: Two Worlds, 1910).

layers of human corruption. Wright argued that whilst philosophy, theology, scripture, and personal mystical experience were important, questions relating to spiritual truth and the immortality of the soul can only be definitively decided through "psychical research" and "scientific proof." Wright believed that psychical research was gradually demonstrating the likelihood of some form of continuity of life after death. However, he rejected dogmatism, suggesting that it was necessary to be open to the possibility of being proven wrong. "The danger," he explained, "lies in our becoming dogmatic," as "dogma has been the cause of the degeneracy of every religious system." "We are Truthseekers," he explained, and "we seek the Truth because we know that the Truth will make us free. As Truthseekers we must keep an open mind to receive it from whatever source it may come ... As it stands at present, Spiritualism is the least dogmatic of all systems: may it ever remain so."[11]

Whilst Wright was sceptical about the value of sacred texts as sources of literal history and meaning, he considered them essential as sources of parables and hidden wisdom. In two articles published in *The Theosophist* (a periodical founded by Helena Petrovna Blavatsky), "The Virgin Birth" (1910) and "The Prodigal Son" (1911), Wright observed that the Essenes and other Christian communities regarded the sacred texts as "parabolical" rather than historical. It was their "spiritual or hidden meaning" rather than a "literal rendering" that was important. This interest in Theosophy continued with two articles in the *Adyar Bulletin*. From there he ranged through the philosophical approaches of Theosophy; thus we should not be at all surprised when some of his earliest Masonic writings are concerned with the Temple of Solomon. Wright believed that for "students of the mysteries of all Scriptures," it was important to look for the "deep substratum of esoteric and occult teaching, some gem buried deep beneath the soil." Wright suggested that corruptions crept into Christianity when people started to read and interpret Christian scriptures as if they contained a literal history. "The Spirit of Truth," he concluded, cannot be directly communicated to the world; "to some it must be presented under the form of parables."[12]

Related to his dislike of dogma, Wright was also concerned about the fate of minorities and their roles in society. Thus we find articles and books on

---

11 Dudley Wright, *Spiritualism in Relation to the Doctrine of Immortality* (Manchester: The Worlds, 1910), 1–14; Dudley Wright, "Can Reincarnation be Demonstrated?," *Occult Review*, (October 1910), 221–27.

12 Dudley Wright, "The Virgin Birth," *The Theosophist*, November 1910, 217–26; Dudley Wright, "The Prodigal Son," *The Theosophist*, March 1911, 927–30.

Woman and Freemasonry (1922),[13] Jews and anti-Jewish prejudice, and on the oppression of Freemasons by the Roman Catholic Church (discussed later).

In addition to "psychical science" and the search for veiled wisdom in the sacred texts, Wright also sought truth in a number of other esoteric and unusual sources. For example, he examined Druidism in a number of articles and a book.[14] He also examined legends and folktales about preternatural creatures, such as vampires and poltergeist. In July 1910, Wright published an essay entitled "A Living Vampire" in the *Occult Review*.[15] The *Occult Review* was a monthly magazine, contributed to by notable writers on the occult, such as Arthur Edward Waite, and published by William Rider & Son. This essay into the world of Vampires resulted in his 1914 book *Vampires and Vampirism* with the same publisher, which is still in print and popular.[16] This relationship with William Rider was to serve both parties well for the next decade, resulting in several other articles published in the *Occult Review*,[17] two books on psychical science,[18] one on poltergeist phenomenon,[19] and at least three on aspects of Freemasonry.[20]

In addition to the occult, spiritualism, and psychical science, Wright also began to take an active interest in Buddhism. He published an article about the

13 Dudley Wright, *Woman and Freemasonry* (London: William Rider & Son, 1922). Such was the impact of this book, it is still today considered a standard text for Co-Masonry.

14 For example: "Druidism and Magic," *Occult Review*, 21:4 (April 1915); "Druidism: Initiatory Rites: Priesthood," *Occult Review* 24:3 (September 1916); "Druidism," *The Freemason*, 17 August 1918)]; "The Creed of Druidism," *The Freemason*, 24 May 1919–28 June 1919; "The Affinity of Druidism with Other Religions," *Open Court*, March 1921; *Druidism: The Ancient Faith of Britain* (London: Ed. J. Burrow, 1924).

15 Dudley Wright, "A Living Vampire," *Occult Review*, 12:1 (July 1910).

16 Dudley Wright, *Vampires and Vampirism* (London: William Rider & Son, 1914).

17 Some examples include "Can Reincarnation be Demonstrated?" (October 1910), "Druidism and Magic" (April 1915), and "An Occult Islamic Order" (December 1923).

18 The aforementioned translated editions of *Psychical and Supernormal Phenomena* (1916) and *Psychic Science* (1918).

19 Dudley Wright, *The Epworth Phenomena* (London: William Rider & Son, 1917).

20 Dudley Wright, *Masonic Legends and Traditions* (London: William Rider & Son, 1921); Dudley Wright, *Roman Catholicism and Freemasonry* (London: William Rider & Son, 1922); Dudley Wright, *Woman and Freemasonry* (London: William Rider & Son, 1922).

role of women in Buddhism in 1911,[21] a book about Buddhism in 1912,[22] and was the editor of the *Buddhist Review* about 1913–1915. He also presented lectures for a course delivered by the Buddhist Society of Great Britain and Ireland. In 1913, in an article about the origins of Buddhism in the *Buddhist Review*, Wright argued that "all religious systems are characterised by the same historical development. There is first the teaching of the truth in purity and simplicity, so far as it can be ascertained; then there is traceable the gradual accumulation of errors, until, sometimes, there appears to be no visible trace of the foundation." It was this unsullied pure and simple foundation that he often seemed to be in search of. Whereas he had previously expressed some scepticism about the major religions, observing that dogma had "been the cause of the degeneracy of every religious system," in 1913 he argued that Buddhism was a relatively pure religion. In other words, he believed that it contained a significant core of truth, and closely approximated the underlying true religion that he sought. He argued that unlike other religions, which he suggested had deviated from the lessons of their original teachers, the fundamental principles of Buddhism have not changed from those taught by Buddha, and thus were not corrupted by human accretions. Wright acknowledged that various accretions had been added to "the foundation," but he contended that "the foundation remains throughout clearly visible." He concluded that Buddhism was "the ultimate of human thought and aspiration, for no religion or philosophy since evolved or propounded has surpassed it either in simplicity or grandeur."[23]

A couple of years later, Wright found himself drawn to Islam, and in 1915, Islam seemed to replace Buddhism in his thinking as the purest of religious systems. He would later contend that Buddhism, unlike Islam, had been corrupted by "the intrusion of a priestly caste."[24] The first of his articles on Islam was published in the *Islamic Review* in August 1915. In this article, he argued that whilst all religious systems have truth at their foundation, "degeneracy" from the original spiritual base was "a characteristic of nearly all religious systems in the history of the world." "Islam," he argued, was the "one religious system in which this downgrade tendency is absent." As he had with Bud-

21 Dudley Wright, "Buddhism and Woman," *Buddhist Review,* 3(1911): 243–50.

22 Dudley Wright, *A Manual of Buddhism* (London: Kegan Paul, Trench, Trübner, 1912).

23 Dudley Wright, "The Origin and Influence of Buddhism," *Buddhist Review,* 5:3 (July-September 1913), 195–201.

24 Dudley Wright, "The Essence and Mission of Religion," *Islamic Review,* January 1919, 13.

dhism, he argued that the principle tenants of Islam "as taught today are precisely what they were when propagated by its founder." By way of contrast, he accepted claims that when Islam was first taught, Christianity had fallen into a state of "abominable corruption," and that the Christian world was marked by constant warfare between "the various factions into which Christianity ... was divided." According to Wright, from the first century of the Christian era until the present day, there has been an ever-multiplying number of Christian "sects and divisions differing from each other on important basic principles." "Into the midst of all this confusion," Wright observed, "came the word of God, spoken through Mohammed, teaching, as the very name of Islam signifies, submission to the will of God."[25]

When he wrote this article he was not yet a Muslim, though it seems that he was already attracted not just to Islamic thought but also to Islamic practice. He stated that "in the service of Islam there is perfect freedom, and as one who cannot claim the honour of being numbered among the followers of the Prophet, may I be permitted to say that in following the Islamic rule and practice, as far as environment would permit, I have found joy and delight, and the rule in no way irksome."[26] Before the end of August, he had embraced Islam. In September 1915, the *Islamic Review* reported the conversion of "a well-known editor" who adopted the name "Muhammad Sadiq" as his Muslim name. Whilst he adopted the Muslim name Muhammad Sadiq in 1915, he continued to use the pen name Dudley Wright throughout the next few years of his life as a Muslim.[27] By 1920 he had drifted away from Islam,[28] but in the 1940s he returned and fully committed himself to Islam, and used his full Muslim name, "Muhammad Sadiq Dudley Wright," to sign over twenty articles and a book about Islam.

The Mosque that he joined was a part of the Lahore Ahmadiyya Movement,

---

25 Dudley Wright, "The Spiritual Basis of Islam," *Islamic Review*, August 1915, 407–11.

26 Wright, "The Spiritual Basis of Islam," 407.

27 Most of his articles in the *Islamic Review* in the 1910s appeared under the name Dudley Wright. An exception was: Mohamad Sadiq Wright, "Islamism not Fatalism," *Islamic Review*, February 1919.

28 In the July/August 1919 issue of *Islamic Review* it was noted that Dudley Wright was absent for "unavoidable circumstances" and the September issue stated that the 3:15 pm Sunday "Service, Sermon and Lecture" were "postponed for the present". We cannot guess what was cause and what effect.

a liberal, pacifist, and non-sectarian branch of Islam.[29] He became a regular contributor to the *Islamic Review*, the periodical of the Lahore Ahmadiyya Movement. Wright must have been committed to the study of Islam, as by 1917 he had been accepted as a preacher and lecturer at a mosque and prayer house at 39 Upper Bedford Place.[30]

Wright praised Islam and denigrated "orthodox" Christianity in a series of articles published in the *Islamic Review* between 1915 and 1920. He stated that "the fundamental principles and practices of the various systems of Christianity [are], in many respects, ... in opposition to common sense and the natural dictates of the human heart." Wright rejected as folly the idea that God would "ever become so angry with the human race—His own creation and family—as to demand the sacrifice of one of His sons in order to appease His own wrath." He also rejected the Trinity, observing that it "has no scriptural foundation" and "is opposed to reason." He stated that "it is equally in opposition to human thought and reasoning to imagine the direct incarnation of Deity into humanity, a sudden jump, which ... is in direct contradiction of the fundamental teachings of evolution." Belief in "a Trinity of three persons in one" and "of a god born as an infant of a human mother, ... being crucified as a malefactor because others had transgressed the law which he, as god, had formulated ... to satisfy the requirements of that law," Wright argued, are "doctrines opposed to reason." He concluded that such beliefs "involve the straining of the intellect," are "absurd" and "non-natural." Wright also criticised other Christian doctrines and ideas, such as "the Immaculate Conception," "the infallibility of the elected head of any Church," and "the fate of unbaptized infants or adults." Wright concluded that Islam, conversely, is a natural and rational faith, which "during the centuries of its existence, has not

---

29 The Lahore Ahmadiyya movement has a long history of stressing the common ground in the fundamental teachings of all religions, and recognizing the founders of other major religions (e.g. the Israelite prophets, the Hindu sages, Buddha, and Confucius) as recipients of a universal revelation (albeit with Islam as the perfect manifestation of the truth). Ahmadi Muslims have been treated as deviant heretical unbelievers by many Muslims, and are persecuted in Pakistan and other countries.

30 His address according to the entry for Dudley Wright in the 1917 and 1918 issues of the *Who's Who* was 39, Upper Bedford Place. This was the address of a mosque and prayer house for the Lahore Ahmadiyya Movement. Dudley Wright occasionally delivered the Friday sermon and Sunday lectures at this prayer house in 1918, some of which were subsequently published in the *Islamic Review*. The building has since been demolished and replaced by a University of London building.

been found in opposition to common sense and reason."[31]

The idea of an underlying spiritual foundation to all religions was still important to Wright. Whereas previously he believed that spiritualism, psychical science, and Buddhism were the surest path to Truth, he now believed that Islam was the closet match to the earliest unsullied Ur-religion or "true religion." He observed that Islam was "not a new religion," but rather the uncorrupted version of a pre-existing religion that every prophet had tried to restore after a succession of human corruptions. Mohammed's aim, Wright concluded, was to teach that religion had "repeatedly been corrupted and debased by man," and that the various prophets, such as Noah, Abraham, Ishmael, Moses, and Jesus, "had been sent from time to time at different periods to restore it to its original purity." "It was the belief of Muhammad," Wright observed, "that the only true religion had been revealed to man at the earliest stage in human history, and that such religion inculcated the direct and spiritual worship of the one true and only God, the Creator of the universe, the King of all the worlds." It was this earliest "only true religion" that Wright sought, a kind of universal Ur-religion from the "earliest stage in human history."[32]

It is not entirely clear when Dudley Wright drifted away from Islam, but his essays in the *Islamic Review* in 1920[33] were his last positive articles about Islam until he returned to Islam in the 1940s. He wrote an article about Islam in 1924, but it was relatively ambivalent. This would suggest that he abandoned Islam at some point between 1920 and 1924. He was critical of "a certain section of Moslems" who oppose membership in Masonic lodges (which might suggest that his Freemasonry had been reproached by some Muslims), and whereas previously he had argued that Islam was relatively monolithic and unchanging, and hence protected from human corruption, he now argued that Islam and Islamic texts were as divided, splintered, and vulnerable to human interference as orthodox forms of Christianity and the

---

31 See Dudley Wright, "The Naturalness of Religion," *Islamic Review*, September 1915, 450–53; Dudley Wright, "The Islamic Conception of Deity," *Islamic Review*, May 1916, 194–96; Dudley Wright, "Characteristics of True Religion," *Islamic Review*, June 1916, 259–63; Dudley Wright, "Islam and Idolatry," *Islamic Review*, July 1916, 305–308; Dudley Wright, "The Character of Muhammad," *Islamic Review*, February 1920, 50–56.

32 Dudley Wright, "The Spiritual basis of Islam," *Islamic Review*, August 1915, 407–11; Dudley Wright, "Characteristics of True Religion," *Islamic Review*, June 1916, 260–61.

33 See for example, Dudley Wright, "The Character of Muhammad," *Islamic Review*, February 1920.

Hebrew and Christian Scriptures.[34]

FREEMASONRY (1912–1932)

1912 was the year in which Dudley Wright became "a poor Candidate in a state of darkness." On the 20th November 1912 he was initiated into Free-masonry in Eccleston Lodge No. 1624.[35] This was to mark another step in his search for more light, to cause his writing to blossom, and in a some-what haphazard way provide a freelance occupation and an income for the next two decades. Maybe his interest in Theosophy prompted this step into Freemasonry, or it might possibly have been his contacts with A. E. Waite or others through the *Occult Review.*

The next step was the conventional one, that of being Exalted in a Royal Arch Chapter. Thus he became a Companion in Eccleston Chapter No. 1624 in October 1913. By 1919 his membership of Eccleston Lodge was ceased (i.e. NPD), but he rejoined in May 1928. His membership was ceased again in 1932, around the time he converted to Roman Catholicism (discussed lat-er). He also joined Wellesley Lodge No. 1899 in March 1928, but that mem-bership ceased in 1931. The consecration of Fratres Calami Lodge No. 3791 in 1917 clearly attracted Wright for he set out his stall by writing a number of articles for their short lived periodical, the *Masonic Secretaries' Journal*. It was a requirement of this lodge that all members were secretaries and Wright claimed to satisfy that by being the Assistant Secretary to the Cray's Valley Lodge of Instruction which actually met outside London (in West Kent). He was elected and became a member of Fratres Calami Lodge on 30th Septem-ber 1918.[36] We note that in 1920 he was appointed as its Assistant Secretary.

He also became a member of Tuscan Lodge of Mark Masons No. 454 which met in London. For whatever reason Mark Masonry must have held some special pleasure for him because it was the only order in which he became a Master—presumably in Tuscan Lodge. Later he went on to join Valentia Mark Lodge in 1924 which met in Wokingham and to be a founding member

---

34 Dudley Wright, "The Secret Cults of Islam," *Open Court,* July 1924, 432–33.

35 Dudley Wright was initiated on 20 November 1912, passed on 15 January 1913, and raised on 12 February 1913. The lodge met at The Criterion, Piccadilly, London, so presumably dining costs would have been fairly costly by the standards of the day.

36 His name appears on a list of brethren elected as members of the lodge on 30 September 1918. The list was published in the periodical of the Fratres Calami Lodge. See *The Masonic Secretaries' Journal,* 2:6 (January 1919), 335.

Joseph Fort Newton. Kadgihn Studios, Cedar Rapids, Ia.
Courtesy of the Grand Lodge.

of Vaudeville Mark Lodge No. 801 and which met at Mark Masons" Hall in London and was appointed as the founding Director of Ceremonies.[37] Also he was Provincial Assistant Secretary for the Mark Province of Berkshire and Oxfordshire for the years 1927–28.

By 1919, he was arguing in *The Eleusinian Mysteries & Rites*, published by the Theosophical Publishing House, that at one time these mystery religions were the principle vehicle for the existence of religion throughout the world, and that without them the very idea of religion may have died out. He suggested that the rituals of Freemasonry were probably based on these ancient mystery religions, and in particular the Eleusinian Mysteries.[38] Wright also argued in *The Ethics of Freemasonry* (1924) that in some respects Freemasonry was purer and superior to the modern religions of the world. He stated that

> there are some brethren who would place Freemasonry among the religions of the world. To do this is to belittle our Craft. Religions divide men, but Freemasonry is a unifier, not a divider. It soars far higher than any of the religious systems that have found a home among the dwellers on earth. Within its temple there gather together for one common aim and object, Jew and Gentile, Moslem and Buddhist, Parsi and Confucian, ignoring, because forgetting, the divisions that will separate them when they leave the shelter of the sacred fane.[39]

The years 1917 and 1918 were years of considerable Masonic literary progress for Wright. The first visible aspect of this was to appear in print in *The Builder* in November 1918 and was entitled "Masonic War Work in England." Wright says in his introduction to the piece that Joseph Fort Newton had asked him to write it. Quite how this came to happen remained hidden from us until we discovered Newton's description of their first meeting at a 4 July 1916 dinner at Freemasons Hall, Great Queen Street, London.

---

37 This was reported in *The Times*, 9 April 1924, p. 11, col. C. One should not be surprised at this as Wright was the Masonic Editor of *The Times*.

38 Dudley Wright, *The Eleusinian Mysteries & Rites* (London: Theosophical Publishing House 1919). An earlier draft of this book was published serially as Dudley Wright, "The Eleusinian Mysteries," *The Freemason*, 4 January 1919–3 May 1919.

39 Dudley Wright, *The Ethics of Freemasonry* (Washington: MSA, 1924), 28.

Only Freemasonry could have so welcomed a young man in a strange land, made him feel at home, and given him a token of regard for work done in behalf of the Craft. In the less formal hour following the banquet, I met men I had long wanted to know, among them Brother Robbins, President of the Board of General Purposes, Brother Thorp of Leicester, Brother Sir John Cockburn, Brother Songhurst, Brother Churchward, who traces Masonry back a million years or more; Brother Dudley Wright of "The Freemason" and Brother Waite, to whom I am so deeply in debt as teacher and friend. We had much happy talk, and a downright good yarn besides.[40]

Newton's words indicate that his correspondence with Wright was of some standing. It was eventually discovered in a later and seemingly unrelated article in *Masonic News* that at the end of 1927 Wright had told a friend that his association with *The Freemason* had lasted sixteen years; that would indicate that he had worked at *The Freemason* since about 1912/13.[41] Thus his correspondence with Newton, then Editor of *The Builder* could have started almost from its launch.

And with those words Wright became part of what turned out to be seen, in the light of passing decades, as the greatest flowering of American Masonic journalism. This somewhat surprisingly came out of the midwest state of Iowa, and had its heyday starting with the first issue of *The Builder* by the National Masonic Research Society in 1915 until around 1924. There can be little doubt that this greatly influenced Dudley's writing. The tale is both unusual and little known on either side of the Atlantic, and is thus worth relating.

NATIONAL MASONIC RESEARCH SOCIETY & *THE BUILDER* MAGAZINE (1913–1925)

It might seem unlikely that the town of Cedar Rapids, in rural agricultural Iowa, should have become a centre of Masonic excellence. Equally that the

---

40 Joseph Fort Newton, "British Freemasonry: A Diary of Fellowship," *The Master Mason*, January 1924, 30

41 Herbert F. Inman, "Why I Resigned," *Masonic News*, 27th May 1929, 416–17. Thus it seems likely that the financial difficulties of *The Standard* and joining *The Freemason* left Wright with at least some income.

library and museum on First Avenue, Cedar Rapids,[42] probably ranks among the best five Masonic libraries in the world. It was a resolution of Grand Lodge in 1840 that the Grand Secretary be allocated funds to purchase books. The library was first located in the home of Theodore S. Parvin, the first librarian. It has since grown and became in 1884 the first Masonic library to have its own purpose built facility.

In 1913 a Committee on Masonic Research was set up and in 1914 it reported to Grand Lodge. They were authorised to "take steps to organise a National Society of Masonic Research" and Bros. George L. Schoonover, N. R. Parvin, and Joseph Fort Newton set about the task with energy. What the endorsement of such a plan by the Grand Lodge of Iowa meant in the Masonic world, is at once evident, as witnessed by these words by Chetwode Crawley (whose distinguished services to Masonic scholarship in England no student needs to be told):

> Let me begin by expressing my deep satisfaction that the Grand Lodge of Iowa has extended its sanction to Masonic Research by the appointment of so influential and capable a committee as that indicated in your letter ...

> ... For more than a generation, we have been accustomed to see the Grand Lodge of Iowa leading the van in the cultivation of the literature of Freemasonry.[43]

Bro. George Schoonover had become enthused by the fact that among the almost two million masons in the United States were a growing number who sought knowledge. He became convinced that what the Craft in America needed was something that was national rather than local and also something that was not an official publication of any one grand lodge. He settled upon the concept of a monthly journal, well edited and printed, illustrated, without advertisements, and produced to the same standards as non-Masonic journals. It would be subscribed to by individual brothers for an annual fee

42 The library contains over 100,000 books, not all Masonic; and also a massive card index to all articles in the vast collection of Masonic magazines mostly but not all from the United States. Researchers are welcomed by Bro. Bill Krueger and his team and there is a steady trail of visitors to this mid-west treasure.

43 Joseph Fort Newton, "A Foreword." This comment by the noted Irish Freemason and researcher Chetwode Crawley in the first issue of *The Builder*, January 1915, The National Masonic Research Society. It both marks the connections Newton had across the Masonic world and very much sets the international tone of the magazine.

of $2.50 (later to become $3.00).

The Builder

A Journal For The Masonic Student

Published Monthly by the National Masonic Research Society

VOLUME VI
NUMBER 12   December, 1920   TWO DOLLARS FIFTY CENTS THE YEAR
TWENTY-FIVE CENTS THE COPY

Schoonhover took his ideas to the Grand Lodge of Iowa who endorsed it. He proceeded to build a headquarters for the magazine in his home town of Anamosa (some twenty-five miles south of Cedar Rapids), employed Joseph Fort Newton as editor-in-chief, and the first issue went out on 1 January 1915. Membership grew steadily, eventually with hundreds in other countries (and 200–300 in England alone) reaching something in excess of 20,000 copies. While the society had its own "managing Board of Stewards" it also had a team of associate editors to support Newton—Harry Leroy Haywood, Jacob Hugo Tatsch, Robert I. Clegg, Louis Block, A. B. Skinner, and Dudley Wright.[44]

Such was the success of *The Builder* that its name still lives on, and indeed in the early days of the internet (in the mid-1990s) when bandwidth was narrow and the ability to create PDFs was rare, the whole series was converted into Microsoft Word and then HTML.[45]

---

44 Upon the departure of Newton to London, Haywood became unpaid editor for two years, eventually leaving in 1924 to take the job of editor of the *New York Masonic Outlook* (the *Outlook* was supported by the Grand Lodge of New York, had a long life, and under Haywood's editorship had some specially commissioned stunning art deco covers. Tatsch became assistant editor for a year before leaving and was succeeded by R. J. Meekren, who became editor in chief in 1925

45 *The Builder* in text can be found at http://www.phoenixmasonry.org (accessed March 2014). Assuming that the transcription is correct, the simple fact that all the page formatting has been removed and the relative importance of materials on a page is lost. Its transcription was the work of George Helmer in the 1990s, before his tragic death in 2002.

Dudley Wright's first article in *The Builder*[46] was "Masonic War Work in England" in the November issue of 1918, and he was to continue writing around ten articles each year until his final article "John Theophilus Desaguliers" in the March 1924 issue. The questions are, how did he become known to *The Builder* and become an active contributor of editorials, and then why, in full flow, did that suddenly stop in 1924?

Joseph Fort Newton was born on 21 July 1876 in Decatur, Texas, the son of a Baptist Minister, and he attended the Southern Baptist Seminary and then Harvard University. He was ordained in 1895 and held pastorates in Texas and then non-sectarian Universalist Congregations in Illinois and then Iowa. It was in Illinois that he was initiated in 1902 into Friendship Lodge No. 7. In 1908 he became Pastor of the Liberal Christian Church in Cedar Rapids, and that post held him until he left in 1916.

Many of his sermons were published and read both in England as well as in the USA. The quality of these must have been truly exceptional because in 1916 he was invited to the pulpit of the City Temple in London where he eventually decided to stay till 1920. The City Temple, now on Holborn Viaduct (since 1874) in London was the centre of Nonconformity in the City of London, and its pulpit one of very considerable status.

The previous pastor of the City Temple, R. J. Campbell, resigned in 1915 and shortly afterwards Newton received a request from *The Christian Commonwealth* (the house paper of the City Temple) to print his sermons. A little later he got intimations from friends that he would be called. He records that "a cablegram arrived from the Board of Deacons asking me to spend a month preaching in the City Temple. Since it was only for a month I accepted." He does not say it but reading his *Diary of Fellowship* it is clear that the urge to

---

46 He was described as being the assistant editor of *The Freemason*, London. The opening sentences are:

Brother Dr. Fort Newton has honored me with the request that I should put on paper some particulars of what the brethren in England are doing toward the relief of the distress and suffering brought into being through this terrible war and what steps they are taking to bring about, in an honourable manner, the end toward which all eyes are turned. The task is not an easy one for the very reason that Brother Fort Newton himself gave only a few days since at the City Temple. English people do not advertise, except it be to announce in a loud voice the indiscretions they commit. Particularly is this so of the brethren of the Craft in England. I have frequently met brethren who have almost shuddered when they have seen the report of a Masonic gathering in the secular press. "Oh, how wrong!" has been their exclamation. It is, perhaps, unnecessary for me to say that I make them shudder as often as I can. There are members of the Craft who refuse to subscribe to Masonic journals on the ground that they are unnecessary and ought to be abolished. But possibly there may be another explanation of this refusal.

The Little Brick Church, Cedar Rapids, Iowa, where Joseph Fort Newton held the pulpit. Courtesy of Cedar Rapids Historical Society and thanks to Bill Kreuger, Iowa Masonic Library.

visit the British Isles was strong, the call of the places of American history, Shakespeare's home town, and his Masonic friends making this an opportunity not to miss. His diary was packed full for the month! In his autobiography, *River of Years*, he records the tensions between the deacons and the church. As the month ended he sailed for home undecided and eventually wrote a letter declining but with the caveat "that if they could not find anyone else to do what was needed at the City Temple, I would try my best." In the end, only the postscript was read to the church as he discovered one day when picking up his local paper only to read that he had accepted—"The die was cast," were his words. The most controversial thing about the invitation to Newton was not his theology, nor his Baptist background, but the simple fact that he was an American. The congregation called him and he came, and his position was made permanent.

Little seems to have been written about any interaction between the Masonic intellectuals of England and the members of the National Masonic Research Society. It is clear that there must have been an active exchange between both groups, and one of them, the Englishman Dudley Wright, was to become an associate editor from pre-1918 to 1924. He became firm friends with Newton, whose words speak quite loud enough:

> MEANTIME, I have written an introduction to a little book about the Eleusinian Mysteries, by Brother Dudley Wright, a dear gracious, brotherly man, who reminds me of Dr. Johnson and knows more about things old, odd, and interesting than any man has a right to know. He is a perpetual delight, as much for his loyal good-will as for his wide learning, and his friendship is sweet.[47]

Much of Newton's effort went into encouraging Anglo-American support for the war efforts and there are even articles recounting the Masonic support for individuals damaged by the war. Dudley Wright's views on the role of women was not dissimilar to Newton's for his book *Woman and Freemasonry* became a classic, and he also had an article on the same topic in suffragette magazine *The Englishwoman*,[48] which also contained a piece by Maude Royden (who Newton had controversially appointed as his assistant at the City Temple).

47 J. F. Newton, "British Freemasonry: A Diary of Fellowship," part 11, *The Master Mason*, November 1924, 775.

48 D. Wright, "Woman and Freemasonry," *The Englishwoman* (December 1920), 214–19.

City Temple, London (2014). Jack1956, Wikimedia Commons.

It is worth mentioning Newton's Universalist Church of America affiliation. The church emerged in 1793 in the USA and peaked in the 1830s when it was the ninth largest denomination in the United States. Among its social and political stances were abolitionism, separation of church and state, an acceptance that some members were sympathetic to spiritualism, and the ordination of women The church still exists as the Unitarian Universalist Church.49 It is a liberal religious association who see themselves as a separate religion with its own beliefs and affinities. They define themselves as non-creedal, and draw wisdom from various religions and philosophies, including Humanism, Christianity, Hinduism, Buddhism, Judaism, Islam, and Earth-centred spirituality. Given such inclinations it is easy to see why Newton and Wright got on together so well and why they both disliked dogmatism.

Newton returned to the US in 1920, not to Iowa, but first to New York and then to settle in Philadelphia. This almost random event, both in personal and geographical terms, was to greatly affect many things that were both Masonic and American, but also especially the writing outlets for Bro. Dudley Wright.

It had become clear to Newton that it was not possible to continue to edit *The Builder* while he remained in London, and in June 1917 he resigned his editorial post. Harry Leroy Haywood, who some say had effectively already been doing the job for a couple of years, although without any remuneration, formally took over the reins as editor in 1921 until August 1925, with Jacob Hugo Tatsch as assistant in 1922 to 1923. Robert J. Meekren (a Canadian from Quebec) then took over and was the editor until its closure in 1930.

Around this time other things were happening for in January 1923, *The Builder* moved from Anamosa, twenty-five miles west to Cedar Rapids, to premises at 2920 First Avenue. It was duly announced in the January 1923 issue that it was moving and bringing all its equipment and resources of the society with it. Alas this was not to be its only move for it was announced in the September 1923 issue that it was to move to St. Louis, Missouri, and further explanation was given in *The Builder* of November 1923.

All these changes had been occasioned by the departure of Schoonover from the scene. Wherever one reads about Bro. Schoonover, one finds praise for his vision, enthusiasm, energy, and organising ability. However in early 1923 he was accused of "un-Masonic behaviour," six volumes of evidence were

---

49 For information about the current church at City Temple, see http:/www.city-temple.com/ (accessed July 2014).

gathered, and after a (Masonic) trial on 31st May he was found guilty and expelled from the Craft. Thus he departed the Grand Lodge of Iowa, and resigned as executive secretary of the NMRS. All this occasioned the removal of *The Builder* from Anamosa to Cedar Rapids.

After the departure of Schoonover from the post of executive secretary of the NMRS, the position was filled by Frank H. Littlefield. Littlefield was the president of the Standard Masonic Publishing Company and publisher of *The Missouri Freemason*. It was thus perhaps unsurprising to find that *The Builder* and its equipment and resources had moved to St. Louis (although the material resources soon returned to Cedar Rapids). Dudley Wright's last article in *The Builder*, entitled "John Theophilus Desaguliers," was in the March 1924 issue.

Other events of relevance where also happening. The first was the formation of the Masonic Service Association of the United States, the second was the change in structure of the organisation of both the NMRS and *The Builder*, and the third was a feeling in the Craft grand lodges of the United States that they were being increasingly beset by the following sentiment:

> ... we may need a new set of Masonic police regulations that will put these bums in the bastille where they belong.

So ends the article in *The Builder* of November 1923 by Louis Block, PGM, Iowa. The edition that details the move to St. Louis contains the salutatory from Littlefield, and was issued under the new ownership and new board of stewards and the very extended editorial team. But what he has to say in the article with the bland title of "Present Day Tendencies and Dangers in Freemasonry" does deserve our attention. The following abstracted quotes about the Shriners and similar "side orders" perhaps indicate that a change of stewardship meant a change of editorial style and content was going to take place as well.

> ... there have arisen in recent years a number of organisations pretending to be Masonic that are anything but serviceable to mankind.

> We say parading advisedly, for their votaries seem set upon strutting the streets clad in gay, gaudy and garish garment, flaunting

flaming banners, tearing the public peace to tatters with the blare of trombone and the boom of the bass-drum.

These institutions are growing in number. The other day the writer counted up fourteen of them. Grand Masters and Grand Lodge Correspondents have assailed them in no uncertain terms, and not without reason, for they are a real menace to Masonry.

Treating the Blue Lodge degrees as mere stepping stones, they tread beneath ruthless feet the beautiful flowers of the ritual, in a mad effort to rush the candidate into their fold.

These side-orders strive to slur over all these and to substitute in their place a silly seeking for pleasure and a light headed lust for excitement.

It is also worth noting that from its inception in 1915 until 1923, *The Builder* ran with an editor and six or seven associate editors who turned out a monthly magazine—their main strength was that they were all Masonic writers of note who had authored books and articles, and they had, as a team, both depth and strength to make the magazine interesting. The move to St Louis resulted in the loss of some of the editorial team (of which more later), and afterwards the editorial team consisting of an editor and somewhere between fifteen and seventeen associate editors. If one searches these names it becomes clear that the new team does not have anything like the same depth of writing experience as the old one. It perhaps speaks volumes that in 1925 they were actually reprinting articles on the Masonic history of Canadian grand lodges—not a matter likely to excite the subscribing reader one must suspect.

In the June 1984 issue of the *Philalethes* an article on Iowa's Masonic Magazines[50] interestingly states that:

> Note revealed in the pages of *The Builder* was some behind the scenes maneuvering. Former Editor J. F. Newton was in favour of a move to transfer the Research Society and *The Builder* to the Masonic Service Association. He also wrote, in a letter, that the MSA was planning a new magazine which would "knock the spots off *The Builder*." Newton, in fact, became editor of that new magazine, *The Master Mason,* which lived for about seven years.

And among those who would transfer their allegiance to *The Master Mason* were J. Hugo Tatsch and Dudley Wright.

HOW DIFFERENT THINGS MIGHT HAVE BEEN

The ultra conservative tendencies of those in charge of parts of Freemasonry in the United States still crop up from time to time, even today, just as it did in the 1920s. It might be possible to write off Louis Block's article as a mere fit of pique but the tensions he talks of surface elsewhere, even if they only eventually saw the full light of day in the late 1920s and early 1930s.

Block might have issued his tirade against the Shriners, but in many ways he was equally condemnatory of the many "side orders" which poached not only the affiliation of "new" brothers but distracted them from the essential core purpose of Freemasonry—the three degrees and an understanding of them. Block said that, "The other day the writer counted up fourteen of them."

It would be remiss to pass on without some mention of either The Philalethes Society or North Carolina Lodge of Research No. 666 and its correspondence circle, because they both recapture the essence and energy of the

---

50 K. Arrington, "Iowa's Masonic Magazines: The Builder," *The Philalethes,* June 1984. (http://www.tntpc.com/252/philalethes/p84jun.html, accessed March 2014). There is an implication in what Arrington writes that at the time of the move to St. Louis (September 1923) that Haywood mentions "a rather extended illness" which prevented him writing the article planned for the Study Club. This illness eventually forced his resignation from the position of Editor." However Haywood moved to New York and started the *New York Masonic Outlook* for the Grand Lodge of New York. He remained the editor from the first issue in September 1924 till September 1930. Clearly his illness did not prevent him doing a further six years editorship in New York—where Fort Newton was also based and to where J. Hugo Tatsch also removed himself!

It is also worthy of note that a person using the initials HLH advises that there are extensive records of these times in the vaults in Cedar Rapids. This might well repay study by some researcher in the future.

early years of *The Builder* with its enthusiasm for spreading knowledge on the many corners of Freemasonry, but this only crystallised in the 1930s. There seems little doubt that after the "move to St. Louis," *The Builder* lost its essential ebullience and energy, and the end of 1923 began the start of a long and slow decline that ended in 1930 with closure.

The question was how the energies of that small group of enthusiastic exploring and educating masons was to find an outlet. One answer was *The Master Mason* edited by Newton, which continued the style of *The Builder*, and there was its educational equivalent formed in 1928, The Philalethes Society. The first forty Fellows included seven who had been on the editorial team of *The Builder*. However, by the time they named the first set of fellows it was 1931, both *The Builder* and *The Master Mason* had folded, and the Great Depression was still exerting its influence. The fellows thus confined themselves to writing articles and submitting them to other journals for publication, and only in 1948, after the end of World War II, did they actually start their own publication, *The Philalethes*.

Alan E. Roberts however describes the start of the Philalethes rather more dramatically:

> "Petty tyranny gave birth to The Philalethes Society," I wrote in 1988. "Some Masonic leaders," I continued, "dressed in brief authority," had attempted to inhibit the spread of truth. They had attacked, in many cases successfully, the publishing of the written word. They had endeavoured to warp the minds of the greatest intellects in Freemasonry." 51

Founded in 1930, the North Carolina Lodge of Research No. 666 was the first American research lodge and, again, a by-product of attempts to control Freemasonry. Its transactions, *Nocalore*,[52] were published for nineteen years and the lodge closed in 1954. During that time and with the support of a broadly-based correspondence circle, they also had a keen interest in the multitude of extant orders, many of which they imported into the USA. The list includes Allied Masonic Degrees, Operatives, Knight Masons of Ireland, and Knights Beneficent of the Holy City (CBCS). Again two of the team from *The Builder* were involved as active members, J. H. Tatsch and C. C.

---

51 Alan E. Roberts, "The Philalethes Society: Seekers of Truth," *Short Talk Bulletin*, MSA-NA. January 1997. The original appearance of the quote in 1988 has not been traced

52 *Nocalore* simply stands for "**NO**rth **CA**rolina **LO**dge of **RE**search" rather than being a word with any esoteric meaning.

Hunt, together with others such as J. Ray Shute and J. Edward Allen. While one might surmise that there was some link between those in the North Carolina Lodge of Research evidence proved elusive until at last there was an article in Wright's *Masonic News* by J. Ray Shute[53]—this is at least indicative of contact. What all these activities, including the departure of Newton and Haywood, do mark is a passing of the education and research mantle away from Iowa and towards the East Coast.

The Masonic Service Association (MSA)

The American (Craft) Masonic structure based upon states has some clear advantages in such a geographically vast country as the United States; however when there is a need to act collectively, then such a system has great disadvantages. The very idea of a national grand lodge has always been fought tooth and nail by grand lodges, who clearly had status to preserve; though how concord could reign from Rhode Island through New York to Iowa and all the way to California has to remain a big unanswered question. The problem was demonstrated in the First World War when "the boys fighting over there" needed support. The Overseas Mission of the Grand Lodge of New York had provided some Masonic support, but coordination was the big problem.

Schoonover's idea, which he developed with Judge Townsend Scudder, PGM New York, was to create a permanent and continuously active organisation, owned, controlled, and funded by the grand lodges. It would be able to provide a central coordinated point in any time of emergency. It seems the question was how to keep the staff together. The answer was that the proposed association should also provide a program of nationwide Masonic educational services. When Schoonover resigned as executive secretary, his place was taken by Bro. A. L. Randell—and the MSA then moved to the Washington, D.C., area where it is still today (2015). It is interesting to note that the functions set out for it back in 1918 remain pretty much unchanged; it is a clearing house for disaster donations, it has a hospital visitation program (which includes but is not limited to veterans), and it has an educational program in the form of the *Short Talk Bulletins* (which endure to this day having published one bulletin every month for NINETY-TWO years).

Wright contributed thirty-nine articles to the *The Master Mason* mostly in the

---

53 J. Ray Shute Jr, "Ancient Symbols: The Equilateral Triangle," *Masonic News*, 7:157 (Saturday 3 January 1931), 3–4.

first three years, and his work clearly reduced as his time at home got swallowed up in running his own magazine. In 1930 there was just one article, with both magazines closing within a couple of months, presumably casualties largely of the Wall Street crash with the economy not turning around until mid-1933.

THE
MASTER MASON

JOSEPH FORT NEWTON, LITT. D., EDITOR　　　　　　　　ANDREW L. RANDELL, LL. D., MANAGING EDITOR
CARL H. CLAUDY, FREDERICK W. HAMILTON, LL. D., ASSOCIATE EDITORS
ROSCOE POUND, LL. D., HENRY R. EVANS, LITT. D., AND DUDLEY WRIGHT, CONTRIBUTING EDITORS

| VOLUME VI | SEPTEMBER, 1929 | NUMBER 9 |

The editorial team changes reflect the times. Tatsch left in September 1924 and in the following month was replaced by Carl Claudy. The eminent Roscoe Pound remained on the team presumably for his legal opinion, because his written contributions were as small as his reputation for legality and ethics was renowned. By 1927 the pressures of editing a monthly magazine were showing because Carl Claudy and Frederick W. Hamilton were named as associate editors and Henry R. Evans joins as a contributing editor.[54]

The MSA took the decision in early 1929 that its job was not to run a busy Masonic magazine, and the published name in the bottom banner became The American Masonic Press Incorporated instead of the MSA. At the end of 1929 Newton resigned from the post of editor and Randell took his place, but sadly Randell only edited three issues—January, February, and a joint March-April issue—and it then ceased publication.

And thus ended Dudley Wright's American Masonic article-writing employment, which had spanned a full and busy decade. Wright was and is, perhaps strangely, both then and now, held in higher esteem in the United States than in England. This was going to serve him well when it came to the Americanization of his revised Gould's *History*.

---

54 Newton, in the bibliography to his autobiography only lists (with his usual modesty) his editorship of *The Builder* from 1915 to 1916 and of *The Master Mason* from 1924 to 1926. Thus the appearance of Carl Claudy and Frederick Hamilton as associate editors probably means the while Newton's name was on the banner the work was actually done by the associate editors.

While much of the story takes place in the United States, we should not lose sight of the fact that Wright lived in England for all his life, and never even visited the United States. He was not blessed with any private income and had to make his living from his pen. His early career (from 1890 to 1913) remains undiscovered.[55] One hint in his biography in *The Masonic Secretaries' Journal* of September 1918[56] refers to his career as "for many years a member of the editorial staff of the ill fated *Standard* newspaper." What we can know is that the London *Standard* suffered financial difficulties in 1913 and that his work at *The Freemason* in some capacity started in 1912 or 1913. Newton records meeting Wright on the 4th July 1916 and refers to him as "Brother Dudley Wright of *The Freemason*." By 1916 he declares himself to be Assistant Editor; it was however in the nature of the practice of those times that it was only the name of John Denyer Hand, the owner, that appeared as Editor.

THE FREEMASON (1913–1927)

The mainstay of the Wright household economy from 1913 to 1927, together of course with his Masonic work for *The Times*, was *The Freemason*. And yet and in spite of that there is not a vast amount to say about his work at *The Freemason* over fourteen years. The amount of work in filling and putting together a weekly magazine is a major task and requires a lot of the skills used at a national daily paper, and Wright had those skills. What he did not have in 1913 was the breadth and depth of Masonic knowledge to author his own Masonic material—thus it is not until 1918 that he is credited with any authorship in *The Freemason*. Those dates also coincide with his first piece for *The Builder* in November 1918. Even by mid-1916 he must have made an impression in terms of Masonic knowledge and authorship because he had been among those brothers who gathered to greet Joseph Fort Newton in 1916.

---

55 The 1901 Census records him as living on the south coast of England at Littlehampton-on-Sea and working as an Engineers Clerk. By 1908 he had moved to the north London suburb of Hendon, and could easily have worked for a London newspaper while living there.

56 Our Contributors No. 1 Bro. Dudley Wright Phil.B., F.S.P. Assistant Editor of the "Freemason," *The Masonic Secretaries' Journal* (January 1919), 328–29

THE FREEMASON—6th JULY, 1929.

THE FREEMASON

THE MASONIC ILLUSTRATED.

A · WEEKLY · RECORD · OF · THE · PROGRESS · OF · FREEMASONRY

No. 3148. Vol. LXIX.   SATURDAY, 6th JULY, 1929.   REGISTERED AT THE G.P.O.   Price 3d.

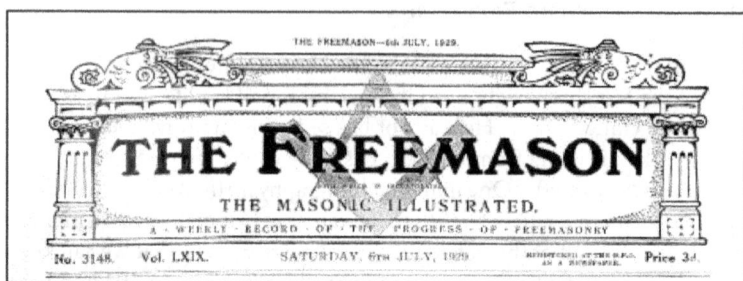

In 1918 Newton invited him to write a piece for *The Builder* and we can only guess what encouragement he gave Wright in terms of Masonic authorship. Wright however had achieved his objective because in 1919 and 1920 he had serialised works on the Eleusinian Mysteries and Rites (seventeen weeks and later published as a book), Druidism (five parts drawn from previous papers), Masonic Legends and Traditions (thirty instalments and later published as a book), and a final thirty-five-instalment work on Roman Catholicism (also later a book). He must have reached some agreement with the owner of *The Freemason* because he was careful that the books were only published after being serialized in *The Freemason*. Any avid reader of *The Builder* will note that articles under similar titles also appear there—Wright was never one to let a good story rest! If one counts all the part works Wright had approximately 175 articles under his name in *The Freemason*.

Masonic News

The timing however proved to be less than opportune to launch a new magazine, because of the economic crisis, and by 1931 publication had ceased and in the Christmas issue of 1929 there was a plea that those subscribers who were late paying or even had not paid at all to part with their money. Wright supplied thirty-two named articles for the 185 issues over three and a half years. The *Masonic News* was very similar in content to *The Freemason*. In a marketing sense it simply did not have a strong enough identity to differentiate it from the competition.

Life after *The Freemason* and *Masonic News* (1927–1931)

There is no doubt that the economic high point for Dudley arrived in 1927, because he was then writing for *The Freemason* and was its editor, and also busy writing for *The Master Mason* in America. *The Freemason* however had slowly become a place where there was an emphasis on bland recitation of events at the United Grand Lodge of Egland, and it was in that sense following the trend set by *The Builder* after 1924. At the end of the day however, and in the years of the Great Depression, this was clearly not going to be a recipe for improving circulation.

The death of John Denyer Hand, the owner and managing editor in January 1927 had left Wright with full, but only acting, editorial control. The banner headline where Hand's name had once been was blank and there was clearly some sort of interregnum. Wright would have been hopeful of gaining the post of editor but he must also have had some reason to suspect that this was not going to be the case. Ultimately in the issue of 17 December 1927 he writes under the heading "PERSONAL" that:

> My connexion with *The Freemason,* which has lasted for sixteen years, will terminate at the end of the present year. For the greater part of that time my services have been of assistant editor and, more recently, as sole editor and manager, and no reason has been given for their abrupt termination. [and he goes on to say] As, however, I step from one editorial chair into another, I hope these happy associations will be continued.[57]

The response was exceptionally rapid. In the next week's issue under the heading "To Our Readers':

> The Proprietors think it is desirable to state that the paragraph which appeared on page 462 of 17th December Issue of "The Freemason" headed "Personal" and signed "Dudley Wright" was inserted without their knowledge, consent or approval, expressed or implied. Bro. Wright's connection with this journal ceased on Monday 19th December.[58]

It seems that there had been or was going to be an announcement of a new editor for *The Freemason* in December, and that it was clear this would not

---

57 Dudley Wright, "Personal," *The Freemason,* 17 December 1927, 462.

58 The Proprietors, "To Our Readers," *The Freemason,* 24 December 1927, 475.

Robert Freke Gould, ca. 1890s, author of the *History of Freemasonry*.

be Wright. The replacement editor was to be Bro. J. J. Nolan.[59] Wright was clearly anticipating this because he had prepared to launch his own *Masonic News* at the start of January 1928.

Masonic News, 1st February, 1930.
LARGEST   CIRCULATION   OF   ANY   MASONIC   WEEKLY

MASONIC NEWS

Vol. V. No. 109.   Saturday, 1st February, 1930.   [   ]   Price 3d.

The Freemason however continued publication,[60] and there were also other well-established competitors. One has to assume that this uphill struggle depleted Wright's bank balance and forced him to eventually close his publication.

MASONIC BOOKS

Dudley Wright was the author of thirty-one books during his life. Of these, fourteen were Masonic and published between 1921 and 1931 with the American edition of Gould's *History* being delayed, although almost certainly written in that time period but published in 1936. He was probably fortunate that he had papers published earlier in the *Occult Review* which was published by William Rider & Son as was his intriguingly titled *Vampires and Vampirism* and his two translations of French language psychical works— they were happy to publish his Masonic works as well.

---

59 J. J. Nolan was later to take up the role of providing *The Times* with its Masonic content. That role had been occupied by Dudley Wright between 1919 and 1933, and J. J. Nolan took over the same year until 1938 just before the outbreak of World War II. Previously Nolan had been editor of the *Rangoon Times* from 1915 to 1925 when he returned to London where he remained it's London correspondent and held a post at the Institute of Journalists

60 After the death of Hand in January 1927, publication was continued by the Administrator of John Denyer Hand, Deceased (vol. 66, no. 3019), and it continued publication until 1951.

THE APOGEE—
1ST REWRITE OF GOULD'S *HISTORY OF FREEMASONRY*

Perhaps the greatest triumphs of the "Authentic School" of Masonic research were the formation of Quatuor Coronati Lodge No. 2076 in London, and the publication of the *History of Freemasonry* under the authorship of Robert Freke Gould, and printing by Thomas C. Jack in Edinburgh. Jack's speciality was illustrated books and purchasing the copyright from Gould allowed him control of the illustrations in the volumes. The printing history of *Gould's History* is sufficiently confusing to have prompted an article in AQC[61] to try to unravel its complexities.

In 1883 Jack had entered into negotiations with John C. Yorston of Cincinnati to publish an American edition. This had come to nothing and there followed a series of "pirate" printings of *Gould's History of Freemasonry*, from the house of Yorston (variously in Cincinnati, New York, and Philadelphia) but Yorston's introduction of additional chapters which reflected the breadth and style of American Freemasonry was essential to generate American interest.

Robert Freke Gould's original masterpiece still stands as a testament of factual detail to this day; however, Gould was a brother who held passionate views. Chapters were required on the subject of the Antients (whom he detested), The Union of 1813 is dispensed with in a mere five pages (because it involved the Antients), and the chapter on Ireland is notably weak. He also lets his views on France become apparent with his chart labelled "Chart of the Chief Perversions of Freemasonry" (After p. 80 in volume 3 of the 3- or volume 5 of the 6-volume series). Some updating was definitely required but who would be the writer to take up his pen and actually edit the words of the maestro Robert Freke Gould?

In the end, and some forty years after the original volumes, Dudley Wright took up his pen to undertake the task. Wright of course had, by the mid-1920s, almost a decade of Masonic enquiry and article writing behind him. The books are entitled *Gould's History of Freemasonry* and are described as "Revised, Edited and Brought Up-to-date by Dudley Wright." There is some further explanation in a publisher's promotional preview abstract volume which states:

---

61 A. R. Hewitt, "R. F. *Gould's History of Freemasonry*: A Bibliographical Puzzle," *AQC*, 85(1972): 61–68.

The super-imposition of the original researches of Dudley Wright on the learning of Gould places the authoritativeness of this new edition beyond any possibility of doubt.

The following page goes on to say that "Its contents are such as to render it almost indispensable to the ordinary Mason." Whether that is a statement "from the heart" or an attempt to recognise the market for potential purchasers is unclear. It is doubtful that Gould would have seen his work as anything other than serious history. However Wright, with his newspaper editorial experience combined with his editorial role at *The Freemason* and with the breadth of his articles, was probably as well prepared as anyone for a task of such magnitude.

Gould in his three (or six) volumes offers the reader 1510 pages, while Wright in his five volume set provides 1454 pages, thus making Wright a mere 3% shorter. When it comes to the degree of being "thoroughly revised and brought up to date," then the changes in volume one of both editions bears joint scrutiny. In summary, Wright edited the 504 pages of Gould (less the chapter on Scotland) into 258 pages, thus covering the same topics in 60% of the pages.

The first chapter on the Ancient Mysteries is reduced by two thirds (in spite of the Essenes being a favoured topic of Wright and the chapters on the Steinmetzen, Corps d'Etat, and Companionage receiving similar cuts). The Old Charges only shrinks by some thirty percent. Tatsch[62] complains that there is more recent work on the Old Charges, such as Knoop and Jones, only mentioned by Wright at the end of the chapter, and he is right. But let us reserve judgment for a while. We have to consider the possibility that the majority of the chapters in volume one of Gould/Wright are all areas, the Old Charges excepted, that had seen no new research discoveries between 1887 and 1931. It feels like an acceptable editorial decision to reduce the page count. What had happened was that between the writing of Gould in the early 1880s and the publication of Gould/Wright in 1931 the accepted Masonic view of our "pre-history" had changed and become less dominant.

---

62 J. H. Tatsch, "Review of Gould's *History of Freemasonry Throughout the World*," AQC 46(1937). Tatsch is reviewing the American edition of Gould/Wright which was published in 1936. He is particularly picky in respect of parts of his review. It is said therefore writing in 1937 referring to Wright in 1924 as having been editor of *Masonic News* in London when he was actually assistant editor of *The Freemason*. He states that the UK edition was published in 1933 when it was 1931. He also states that Wright revised Gould in 1924; it would have been useful to be really certain of that date—but, alas, we cannot be sure.

It is generally acknowledged that Gould's most biased chapters were the History of the Grand Lodge of England According to the Old Institutions (vol. 2 ch. 19), History of the Grand Lodge of England 1761–1813 (especially that part relating to the 1813 Union) (vol. 2 ch. 20), and History of the Grand Lodges of Ireland (vol. 3 ch. 22). The nature of the bias and its amendment by Wright seems worthy of some comment in order to evaluate Wright's revisions. In the chapter on the Antients, Wright restores a proper balance by the use of Henry Sadler's *Masonic Facts and Fictions*[63] and adds five pages on the Royal Arch and in the end gives us fifty-one pages instead of Gould's thirty-one.

In chapter 22 Gould singles out Ireland as having grand lodges (in the plural), strange because England had three or more and Scotland at least two. In a chapter of only eighteen pages Gould takes eleven pages to reach the end of 1731, by which time we read the following:

> In the absence of official documents, therefore, it is difficult to trace even the sequence of Grand Masters, and as the evidence is conflicting,[4] a really trustworthy list of these rulers of the Craft will only be forthcoming when the warrants issued to Lodges between 1730 and 1780 have been diligently examined.

4 The names of those Brethren who are said to have presided over the Irish Craft—derived from both official, and unofficial sources—will be found in the Appendix. [the writer notes that this information is actually NOT in the Appendix to the volume].

Wright of course could rely upon the just published 1925 Lepper and Crossle *History of the Grand Lodge of Ireland*. And his chapter is all the better for that.

GOULD/WRIGHT—
THE AMERICAN EDITION OF THE *HISTORY* (1936)

However the recruitment of Melvin Maynard Johnson (of Massachusetts) and J. Edward Allen (of North Carolina) made it possible to recruit quality writers for a review of every state's Masonic history—a combined opus covering two volumes of the six volume set. Whatever those in England might have thought about Wright and his work, its standard met that of the good

63 Henry Sadler, *Masonic Facts and Fictions: Comprising a New Theory of the Origin of the "Antient" Grand Lodge* (1887; Northamptonshire, England: Aquarian Press, 1985).

and the great of the American Masonic (writing) world who were prepared to be on the title page. This was a popular edition and still easily obtainable secondhand.

The first three volumes of the Caxton edition become the first two volumes of the Scribner edition. Volume four of Caxton becomes volume three of Scribner while the fifth Caxton volume with some amendments to Freemasonry in "the rest of the word" and the addition of ninety-four pages relating to Canada complete the Scribner fourth volume.

The final two volumes of the Scribner edition contain the history of each state grand lodge all set out in alphabetical order finishing with an index of fifty-seven pages. One can do no better that quote Melvin Maynard Johnson in his forward to this final third of the set:

> Never before has the history of American Freemasonry been presented as in this work. No one person could do it. For each jurisdiction, some leader in the Craft, imbued with its spirit and a student of its history, has been chosen to tell the story of that jurisdiction. The tale has thus been told by experts who will be recognised as such by the Brethren of the Grand jurisdictions of which they write. All of them are nationally and some internationally known and acclaimed.
>
> Bro. J. Edward Allen and I have made the selection of the co-authors but we have left them unhampered except by limitations of space. Theirs is the credit for research and the responsibility for conclusions. We are grateful for their co-operation, given freely and without financial reward, but merely that the true story may be told of the Fraternity they love and serve.[64]

Gould presents his writings very much in the form of a listing of facts and a poor index, Wright on the other hand uses the newspaper wordsmith skills to provide a more readable narration and good index. Gould offers extensive footnotes and Wright almost none, each according to their education and professional styles. Today's researcher would probably choose *Ars Quatuor Coronatorum* or *Heredom* for an up-to-date view or more detail.

---

64 D. Wright, *Gould's History of Freemasonry* (New York: Charles Scribner, 1936), 5, foreword.

Both Gould and Gould/Wright offer that good grounding,[65] albeit with perspectives almost half a century apart (and the differences between them do need to be appreciated), and the choice is very much a personal one.

POVERTY AND CIVIL LIST PENSION

One might have thought that both Robert Freke Gould and Dudley Wright might have been able to gain some financial reward from their mighty labours over their "Gould's *History*," Such was not the case. Thomas Jack died before the completion of the series of Gould in 1887. Jack's failed negotiations with Yorston meant that in the absence of any US copyright, Gould ended up with no benefit from the sale of his work in the USA. While Gould was a lawyer one must suspect that his legal practice was adversely affected by his devotion to Masonic history. Whatever the reason, a collection was taken to relieve his poverty and an annuity purchased for him.

Dudley Wright's Masonic writings came to an end in 1931 when the *Masonic News* ceased publication and his Masonic work for *The Times* (of London) also ceased. His British revision of Gould was not greeted with the acclaim he had hoped for, and, for example, was not reviewed in *AQC* or the Masonic press. Wright was not part of the research elite in England and possibly viewed by them simply as a newspaper hack who edited Masonic magazines. The timing of course meant that Wright's revision of Gould was published right in the depths of the world depression that followed the Wall Street Crash of 1929—and the book market would have been greatly depressed. In 1933 we find that he was awarded a Civil List Pension of some £70 per annum (probably equivalent today to some $30,000) by the state, an amount that was increased by 33% in 1938. Such pensions were few, given to maybe around twenty-five people each year for having given some service to the country and who had now fallen upon hard times. Wright was recommended and awarded this though we have not been able to discover whose influence this was due to, but the recommendation would have come from near the centres of power in the nation.

---

65 It is worth noting that a further edition and a series of printings of Gould's *History* was undertaken by the firm of John C. Yorston in Philadelphia. Yorston's version of "Gould's History" used the exact same text as the original version of Gould published by Thomas Jack although he added various chapters to the end under named American authors.

Jews and Judaism (1920–1932)

One religion that interested Dudley Wright was Judaism, which he often praised and linked to Freemasonry and his search for the underlying truth of all religions. For example, in 1920, Wright wrote a short article on the *Sefer Raziel HaMalakh* (the Book of Raziel), a medieval Jewish mystical text containing magical incantations. Wright observed that some believe that this text had been passed down from Solomon to the present day, and he suggested that it was sacred and foundational to both Judaism and Freemasonry.[66] In 1923, he argued that societies of Jewish mystics and rabbis had devoted their lives to "the decipherment of the sacred treasures engraven in symbolical language on the tablets of the Law." He suggested that their love for learning and gnosis had "acted as a vitalizing influence" upon the Jews, and that their discoveries might help to unravel the ancient mysteries.[67] Wright also published a series of essays in the *Masonic News*, *Jewish Guardian*, and *Jewish Chronicle*, and in a booklet, in which he discussed Jews who were Freemasons, criticised anti-Jewish prejudice, and traced connections between the symbolism, myths and legends of Judaism and Freemasonry, which he observed had the Great Temple and Solomon as their source in both cases.[68]

Consistent with his belief that all religious and sacred texts provide insights into foundational core truths, Wright embarked upon a study of the Talmud around 1924.[69] His study resulted in a book in 1932.[70] According to Wright, the purpose of his book was to make the history and contents of the Talmud available to fellow "seekers after truth." Hr praised the Talmud, describing it as "an inexhaustible mine, embodying the purest gold and the most pre-

---

66 Dudley Wright, "The Book of Raziel: A Scarce Jewish Work," *The Freemason*, 21 August 1920, 101. This was republished, with minor revisions, in the *Masonic News*, 27 July 1929, and *Jewish Chronicle Supplement*, October 1931, ii–iii.

67 Dudley Wright, "The Mysteries of Merkabah," *Open Court*, July 1923, 402–407.

68 Dudley Wright, "Jews and Freemasonry," *Jewish Guardian*, 5 October 1923, 10–11; Dudley Wright, "Jews as Masonic Leaders," *Jewish Guardian*, 10 October 1924; Dudley Wright, "Freemasonry," *Jewish Chronicle*, 2 October 1925, 25; Dudley Wright, "Jews and Freemasonry," *Masonic News*, 14 April 1928, 306–307; Dudley Wright, "Some Notes on the Jews in Oxford," *Jewish Chronicle Supplement*, October 1929; Dudley Wright, *The Jew and Freemasonry* (London: 1930).

69 Wright referred to this as yet unpublished book in 1924–25, and published a chapter from it in 1925. See Dudley Wright, "The Burnings of the Talmud," *Open Court*, 39:4 (April 1925).

70 Dudley Wright, *The Talmud* (London: Williams & Norgate, 1932).

cious of stones; its maxims and its ethics instil the teachings of religion and morality of the very highest order." He suggested that "above all, one of the values of the Talmud lies in the fact that it teaches that religion is not a thing merely of creed or dogma, or even faith, but of goodness in activity."[71] The final chapter of the book examined numerous incidents of the confiscation, censorship, and destruction of the Talmud, often sanctioned or commanded by the various Inquisitions, from the thirteenth to the eighteenth century.[72] Dr. Isidore Epstein, a prominent rabbinic scholar, praised this book, and described Wright as one among the "*Chassidé Umot Haolam*" (righteous among the nations). "The general reader," he explained, "will be greatly beholden to him for having spread out before him a wealth of information on the literary and historical side of the Talmud; while Jewish readers will be particularly grateful for the author's admirable and moving survey of the burning of the Talmud."[73]

THE CATHOLIC GUILD OF ISRAEL (1933–1938)

Whilst Wright had something positive to write about most religions, and believed that they all shared the same underlying foundation and core of truth, he was often critical of Catholicism. During the 1920s, Wright published a book and a series of essays in *The Freemason*, *The Builder*, and *The Masonic News*, which criticised Catholicism and condemned Catholic anti-Masonry. According to Wright, the Catholic Church and the popes were determined to employ every means at their disposal to destroy and hurl "papal thunders" at Freemasonry, and to hold Freemasons responsible for wars, revolutions, conspiracies, plots and other crimes.[74]

Considering his acerbic criticisms of Catholicism during the 1920s—which

---

71 Wright, *The Talmud*, 13, 15, 20, 133.

72 Wright, *The Talmud*, 109–132.

73 Isidore Epstein, "The Talmud for English Readers," *Jewish Chronicle*, 7 October 1932, 16.

74 See Dudley Wright, "Secret Societies in the Roman Church," *The Freemason*, 27 November 1920 and 4 December 1920; Dudley Wright, "Roman Catholicism & Freemasonry," *The Freemason*, 8 January 1921–1 October 1921; Dudley Wright, "Secret Societies in the Roman Catholic Church," *The Builder*, 7:4 (April 1921); Dudley Wright, "Roman Catholicism and Freemasonry," *The Builder*, 7:5–12 (May–December 1921); Dudley Wright, *Roman Catholicism and Freemasonry* (London: William Rider & Son, 1922); Dudley Wright, "The First Papal Anti-Masonic Bull," *Masonic News*, 5 May 1928; Dudley Wright, "Roman Catholicism and Freemasonry," *Masonic News*, 10 August 1929.

contrasted starkly to his positive engagements with other religions, such as Buddhism, Islam, Judaism, and Theosophy—Wright's sudden conversion to Roman Catholicism in 1933 is somewhat surprising. Considering his long history of joining various religions as part of his search for shared foundational truths, it would not have been uncharacteristic if he had joined a liberal group within the Catholic Church. However, on 28 October 1933,[75] he joined the Catholic Guild of Israel, an English Catholic organisation which contended that the Catholic Church alone provided the path to truth and salvation. The Guild's primary mission was the conversion of the Jews. Its secondary mission was to educate English Catholics about Jews and Judaism through the publication of articles and booklets. Somewhat unhelpfully for its primary mission, these often repeated anti-Jewish stereotypes, and thus served to deter Jews from joining.[76]

Wright's transition to Catholicism was accompanied by a significant shift in his discourse. It is not clear whether he entirely abandoned Freemasonry when he embraced Catholicism, but he certainly stopped writing articles about it.[77] His ideas about the shared underlying foundation of all religious systems disappeared from his discourse, and whereas previously he had praised Jews, he now criticised them. In February 1934, Wright wrote a letter to Sister Mary Pancratius, the head of the Sister of Sion in London, to explain that he was working on a book which he proposed to call "Judaism v Rome: Pagan and Papal."[78] He enclosed with his letter a draft manuscript for one of the chapters, which was on "the Spanish Inquisition and the Jews." Whilst he had once criticised the Rome and Spanish Inquisitions, in this manuscript he defended them. He repeated traditional stereotypes about Jewish greed, arrogance, and power, and referred to so-called Jewish conspiracies, which he claimed attempted to undermine the Inquisition and murder all the Chris-

---

75 Guild membership book, archives of the Catholic Guild of Israel (henceforth, "CGI Archives'). The CGI archives are held at the Sion Centre for Dialogue and Encounter in London.

76 For more about the Catholic Guild of Israel, see Simon Mayers, "Zionism and Anti-Zionism in the Catholic Guild of Israel: Bede Jarrett, Arthur Day and Hans Herzl," *Melilah*, 10 (2013). For the online edition of this volume, see http://www.melilahjournal.org/p/2013.html.

77 He also allowed his membership in the Wellesley Lodge to cease in 1931; his membership of the Eccleston Lodge ceased on 1 November 1932 as a result of non-payment of dues. The periodical that he owned and edited, the *Masonic News*, came to an abrupt end in July 1931.

78 Letter from Dudley Wright to Sr. Mary Pancratius, 12 February 1934, CGI Archives.

tians in Toledo.[79] Whilst Wright abandoned Catholicism and the Catholic Guild of Israel without finishing his *Judaism v Rome: Pagan and Papal,* he did publish articles and a booklet during his years in the Guild which were presumably intended to be included in the book. In some of these, Wright defended papal edicts against Jews, and suggested that the Talmud—which he had previously praised—and Jewish literature in general, had been rightfully condemned by Catholic authorities, because they contained venomous and false statements about Jesus and Mary.[80]

His Return to Islam (circa 1944–1949)

The reason for Wright's uncharacteristic dalliance with Catholicism and anti-Judaism remains an unresolved puzzle to the authors. Significantly, after he abandoned Catholicism, he soon returned to his old thought patterns, and re-embraced a liberal form of Islam and his belief that all religions contain a core of truth. While it is difficult to pin down the exact dates of this transition, it would seem that Wright abandoned Catholicism and re-embraced Islam and the Ahmadiyya movement sometime between the summer of 1938 and 1944. The intervening years are however a mystery, as Wright published nothing until mid-1944, when he wrote the first of over twenty articles for the *Islamic Review.*[81]

As discussed in the first section of this article, from about 1915 to 1920, Wright had practiced Islam, was accepted as an occasional preacher at a mosque, and had adopted the Muslim name Muhammad Sadiq Dudley Wright. However, during those years, he rarely signed even his Islamic publications with his full Muslim name. In 1944 that changed. He re-adopted the name Muhammad Sadiq Dudley Wright and again became a regular contributor to the *Islamic Review.* This time he used his full Muslim name to sign all of the twenty-two articles he contributed to the periodical from 1944 until his death in 1949.

---

79 Dudley Wright, *The Spanish Inquisition and the Jews,* manuscript, CGI Archives, 36 pp.

80 Dudley Wright, "Some Papal Edicts Against Judaism," *Our Lady of Sion,* 41 (Spring 1934): 9–19; Dudley Wright, *The Catholic Church and the Jews* (Dublin: Catholic Truth Society of Ireland, 1935). See also Dudley Wright, "From Rabbi to Archbishop," *Our Lady of Sion,* 44(Summer 1938).

81 Wright's final published work as a Catholic was Dudley Wright, "From Rabbi to Archbishop," *Our Lady of Sion,* 54(Summer 1938). His next publication was Muhammad Sadiq Dudley Wright, "Futility of Christian Missions," *Islamic Review,* June 1944.

Wright had been critical of "orthodox Christianity" and the doctrine of the Trinity during his earlier Islamic phase. He now re-embraced this discourse. On the one hand he praised the teachings of Jesus, but he suggested that orthodox Christianity had, unlike Islam, declined and departed from Jesus' teachings. "The Word of Truth" as delivered by Jesus, he asserted, "is not lost but it has been smothered by the Christian Church, which is a human and not a divine institution. The Truth, as preached by Jesus, is not to be found in the Christian Church but it is to be found outside Christianity—in Islam, in the Mosque."[82] He argued that the exponents of orthodox Christianity "have preferred ... to follow the will of man as expressed in Papal decrees, synodal discussion and mundane councils, rather than the expressed will of God." "Small wonder," he concluded, "that Christianity has proved so ghastly a failure because it is based upon human frailty and fallacy rather than upon the Divine Will." He argued that "what is sorely needed in the Christian world is the undiluted teaching of Jesus," which is to be found "in Islam."[83]

Whilst he repeatedly argued that Christianity had departed from the teachings of Jesus, his negative representations of Jews and the Talmud seemed to disappear from his discourse, and he noted that Jews and Muslims were alike in sharing "a horror at the doctrine of a Trinity of persons in the Godhead" and rigidly believing in the "Eternal Unity" of God. As he had from 1915 to 1920, he once again argued that Islam "laid down the broad basis of faith in all the prophets of the world and the recognition of truth in all religions." Wright returned to his old belief that Judaism, Christianity, and Islam, as taught by Moses, Jesus, and Muhammad, were not new religions but attempts to purge religion of superstitions and human corruptions, in order to return to the original foundation. He argued (as he had previously as a Freemason) that all the "great religions of the world," despite human corruptions and accretions, "have Truth for their base and that at base, ignoring idiomatic expressions, they are practically identical."[84]

---

82 Muhammad Sadiq Dudley Wright, "The Decline of Christianity," *Islamic Review*, June 1946, 223.

83 Muhammad Sadiq Dudley Wright, "Desperate Christians," *Islamic Review*, September 1946, 311. See also Muhammad Sadiq Dudley Wright, "Muslims Arise! A Call to Action!," *Islamic Review*, May 1946, 164, and Wright, "Futility of Christian Missions," 197.

84 Wright, "The Futility of Christian Missions, 199–200; Muhammad Sadiq Dudley Wright, "The Uniqueness of Islam," *Islamic Review*, November 1944, 314; Muhammad Sadiq Dudley Wright, "The Missions of Jesus and Muhammad," *Islamic Review*, February 1945, 58–60; Muhammad Sadiq Dudley Wright, "Prophethood in Judaism and Islam," *Islamic Review*, December 1947, 447.

As he died in 1949, it is difficult to say whether he found in Islam—or would have found given more time—the spiritual Truth and religious foundation that he so passionately sought, or whether given a little more time, he would have yet again turned to another religious system. However, the tone of one of his final essays, an eighty-year retrospective published in February 1948, would suggest that he was happy with his decision to return to Islam, though he noted that the development of religious thought, pursued "in recognition of the demands of Allah, the Lord of All the Worlds," is not an easy one. Perhaps paraphrasing Rabbi Tarfon, a learned Jewish scholar who lived in the years following the destruction of the Second Temple in AD 70, Wright concluded that "the work is hard but yet the labour is sweet, as are the rewards."[85]

CONCLUSION

This research was also an emotional ride as bit by bit more and more of the printed words unraveled the hidden history of Dudley Wright. At first glance he appeared as perhaps a lonely figure who found solace in his words. However, he was more than a casual writer, as the length of his bibliography and his numerous editorships and affiliations clearly demonstrate. His lifetime journey, seeking light, perhaps exposes Dudley Wright more than most men. Many of us search for spiritual light, but very few follow the path so assiduously and commit those wanderings to print.

Certain aspects of Dudley Wright's life remain a mystery, but clearly that during the second half of his life, from about 1906 to 1949, he was engaged in a passionate quest to find the underlying truth and shared foundation of all religious systems. From 1906 to 1920 he wrote essays, articles and books about the occult, theosophy, spiritualism, supernatural phenomena, myths and legends, the Temple of Solomon, Buddhism, Islam, and Freemasonry. He embraced Buddhism and Freemasonry in 1912, and Islam in 1915. For Wright, there was nothing at all wrong or contradictory about being affiliated and engaged with multiple belief systems simultaneously. As his biographical entry in the *Masonic Secretaries' Journal* in January 1919 explained, he was trying to trace the unvarying foundation of all religious systems. He maintained this open, pluralistic, and non-sectarian stance throughout the 1920s, adding the study of Jewish texts to his repertoire of religions. In the 1930s he

---

85 Muhammad Sadiq Dudley Wright, "Fourscore Years: Retrospect," *Islamic Review*, February 1948, 47–52. Rabbi Tarfon had stated words to the effect that the day is short, the work immense, the labourers slow, the rewards great, and the Master of the House is waiting.

had a brief dalliance with Roman Catholicism and the Catholic Guild of Israel, an ultramontane organisation dedicated to the conversion of all Jews. This was uncharacteristic of Wright, as previously he had acerbically criticised Catholicism and "orthodox" Christianity in a number of books and articles. Furthermore, whereas previously he had written about and praised Judaism, Freemasonry, Islam, and a wide range of other religious systems, after his conversion to Catholicism he only wrote about Judaism (to criticise it) and Catholicism (to praise it). All other religions and belief systems disappeared from his discourse. The reason for this sudden rejection of a broad-minded, theosophical, Masonic, non-dogmatic, pluralistic approach to religion is difficult to explain. It is a puzzle that the authors of this article have not been able to unravel. However, in the 1940s, Wright abandoned Catholicism, and re-embraced Islam and the idea that all religions share the same core truths and underlying foundations.

With the exception of his six years in the Catholic Guild of Israel, Wright's anti-dogmatism remained essential to his being throughout his literary life, as much when he turned eighty as when forty. He was active in attempts after the end of World War I, which failed, to rebuild a more equitable Masonic fraternalism in Europe. His open-minded tolerance of all religions extended to others forms of minorities as well, as he was a keen advocate of the suffragette movement and the rights and participation of women in Freemasonry and religion. Such views were radical in the 1920s.

His philosophical approach to life was very similar to that of Joseph Fort Newton, which is perhaps why their friendship endured. The story is also of cooperation between brothers across the Atlantic but also of a striving to maintain values of toleration and reason. Life is a journey, something amply demonstrated by the unearthing of the life of Dudley Wright.

★

The death has taken place, in a London Hospital, at the age of 81, of Bro. Dudley Wright who may be remembered by the older generation, as once a prominent writer on Masonic subjects, as also the editor of the long defunct 'Masonic News,' the ephemeral and at times regrettably polemical existence of which he launched, after being for some years Assistant Editor of 'The Freemason.'

Of striking Johnsonian appearance, and somewhat close likeness to the late G. K. Chesterton, he had considerable literary ability which he applied in diversified ways, being successively tutor, journalist, and even becoming for a time a Nonconformist Minister, before being a Lecturer and author. Born at Chelsea, he was educated at Ware, and afterwards at King's and University Colleges. He held the degree of Doctor of Philosophy.

Apart from his association with the Craft in editorial capacities and as the author of a number of books and Lodge histories, he took no active interest, retaining throughout the rank of only a Master Mason, although he reached the Chair in a Mark Lodge, a rather puzzling feature on the part of one engaged in some aspects of Masonic research in which he would have been helped materially by progression in office. In later years, he favoured the occult sciences and became also connected with the Roman Catholic press, and afterwards Christian Science.

★

The Freemason's Chronicle, 9 April 1949.

47

BIBLIOGRAPHY

Sweet Memories: Valse. London: W. Paxton, 1905. This item contains seven sheets of music. The item itself is undated, but according to the British Library catalogue, it was printed in 1905. No other record of this item has been found so it has proven impossible to verify this date. It has also proven impossible to confirm with certainty that it was written by our Dudley Wright (as opposed to one of the others—see disambiguation page).

The Fourth Dimension (1906)**

Was Jesus an Essene? 14 Kenilworth Ave, Wimbledon, and Kansas City, MO: Power-Book Co, 1908. 57pp. Related to the Unity Publishing Society and part of the "New Life Booklets" series, this book was published with a preface by Samuel George, the director of the Society of Students of New Life, and a champion of the "New Thought" movement. Three other publications by Dudley Wright are mentioned in the Power-Book catalogue at the end of the book: "The Origin of the Universe", "The Origin of Spiritual Man," and "the Origin of Sin". Copies of these have not been found. They were each priced in the catalogue at 1s. 2d. It was the same price as "Was Jesus an Essene?", and it is thus tempting to speculate that they were booklets of a similar length.

The Rationale of Spiritualism (1910), Untraced*

Spiritualism in Relation to the Doctrine of Immortality. Two Worlds Publishing Company, 1910. 14pp.

Jollivet-Castelot, Francois. *How to be an Alchemist.* Translated by Dudley Wright. William Rider & Son, 1910. Recorded in the *Literary Year-book and Bookman's Directory* (vol. XV), New York, 1911. It has not proven possible to locate this item. It is possible that it was translated but never published. The original volume by Francois Jollivet-Castelot was published in 1897 under the title *Comment on Devient Alchimiste.* *

A Manual of Buddhism. London: Kegan Paul, Trench, Trübner, 1912.

Prayer. London: Theosophical Publishing Society, 1912. 65pp. This book was published with an introduction by James L Macbeth Bain.

Vampires and Vampirism, London: William Rider, 1914. Reprinted in 1924. A number of recent reprints can be found for this still popular item, including *The Book of Vampires.* (Causeway Books, 1973) and by (Thornhill, PA: Tynon Press, 1991). archive.org/details/b24876549

Joire, Paul. *Psychical and Supernormal Phenomena: Their Observation and Experimentation.* Translated by Dudley Wright. London: William Rider & Son, 1916; New York: Frederick A Stokes Co, 1918. This item was listed in the 1910 Rider Catalogues a work in progress. It would thus seem there was a six-year delay in publishing. https://archive.org/details/psychicalsuperno-00joirrich

Boirac, Emile. *Psychic Science: An Introduction and Contribution to the Experimental Study of Psychical Phenomena.* Translated by Dudley Wright. London: William Rider, 1918. Note: Wright lists this book in his 1913 *Who's Who* entry with the title "Psychology of the Unknown". The original French text (online at Gallica) was entitled *La Psychologie inconnue: Introduction et contribution à l'étude expérimentale des sciences psychiques* (Paris, Libraires Félix Alcan, 1908). This item should not be confused with another very similar book by Emile Boirac, translated by W. de Kerlor, with the almost identical title: *Our Hidden Forces ("La Psychologie inconnue"): An Experimental Study of the Psychic Sciences* (New York: Frederick A Stokes, 1917). The introduction implies that the Kerlor text, like the Dudley Wright text, is also a translation of *La Psychologies Inconnue.* This is not the case. Some of the chapters of the two books are the same, though the ordering is somewhat different. It seems that Boirac used chapters written between 1893 and 1903 (a statement to this effect being made in the Hidden Forces book) to create a series of books on an almost identical subject.

https://archive.org/details/psychicsciencein00boiruoft

https://archive.org/details/ourhiddenforcesl00boirrich

The Epworth Phenomena. London: William Rider, 1917; Philadelphia PA: McKay, 1920.

The Eleusinian Mysteries & Rites. London and Denver: The Theosophical Publishing House, 1919. archive.org/details/eleusinianmyster00wrig

Studies in Islam and Christianity. Woking: Woking Muslim Mission & Literary Trust, 1919. A revised edition was published in 1946 under the name

Muhammad Sadiq Dudley Wright. aaiil.org/text/books/others/misc/stud-iesislamchristianity/studiesislamchristianity.shtml

Masonic Legends and Traditions. London: William Rider, 1920.

Robert Burns and Freemasonry. Paisley: Alexander Gardner, 1921. archive.org/details/cu31924013447671

Roman Catholicism and Freemasonry. London: William Rider, 1922.

Woman and Freemasonry. London: William Rider & Son, 1922.

Druidism: The Ancient Faith of Britain. London: Ed. J. Burrow, 1924. archive.org/details/druidismancientf00wrig

Elias Ashmole. London: The Freemason, 1924. 35pp.

"Ethics of Masonry." In *The Little Masonic Library* (Vol. 16). Washington DC: Masonic Services Association of United States, 1924. In the later consolidated reprints published by Macoy Publishing and Masonic Supply Co Inc, this becomes part of Volume 4.

Chips from a Mason's Quarry (1925). Untraced but listed in Wright's 1926 *Who's Who* entry*

England's Masonic Pioneers. London: George Kenning, 1925.

The Masonic Who's Who. London: A Lewis, 1926.

History of Henry Muggeridge Lodge No. 1679 (1927). The lodge was founded in 1877 – a 50th anniversary history.

Select Bibliography of the Works of Israel Abrahams, originally published as a chapter in the "Israel Abrahams Memorial Volume." In *Jewish Studies in Memory of Israel Abrahams.* New York: Press of the Jewish Institute of Religion, 1927. Subsequently reprinted from the memorial volume as a stand-alone booklet by Adolf Holzhausen's Successors in Vienna in 1927.

Robert Burns and his Masonic Circle. London: Cecil Palmer, 1929. Reprinted by Folcroft Library Editions, Folcroft, PA in 1978.

The Jew and Freemasonry. London: Masonic News, 1930. 24pp.

Gould's History of Freemasonry (5 volumes). Edited by Dudley Wright.

London: Caxton, 1931.

History of Home County Lodge No. 3451, Province of Surrey 1910-1931. London: Press Printers, 1931. 40pp.

The Talmud. London: Williams & Norgate, 1932.

Holy Year: April 2, 1933, to April 2, 1934. London: Washbourne and Bogan, 1933.

The Catholic Church and the Jews. Dublin: Catholic Truth Society of Ireland, 1935. An extended version of this booklet was republished in 1944 (again by the Catholic Truth Society of Ireland).

Gould's History of Freemasonry (6 volumes). Edited by Dudley Wright. New York: Charles Scribner Sons, 1936. It is available online from several sources (though the 1931 edition is not online at all) and a search should find it with ease.

History of Naturism (1937). According to his *Who's Who* entry, he published this volume under the pseudonym Patrick Mcnulty. This is the only item that Dudley Wright apparently published using this pseudonym (though it is possible that he published other items using other pseudonyms or anonymously, which may explain the difficulty locating certain items). A copy of this item has not been found. Significantly, a link would seem to exist between this pseudonym and his mother's maiden name, which was Jane McNulty.*

Jesus, Judas and Pilate (1937). Untraced.*

Five Pillars of Islam (1946). This is listed in Dudley Wright's *Who's Who* entry as if it was a book, but a copy of it has not been found. However, an article with this name can be found in the *Islamic Review* for 1946. It is possible that the entry in the *Who's Who* simply refers to this article, but it is also possible that the article was also published as a pamphlet. Untraced.*

> *Some titles could not be traced by the authors (as of 2016) but they are left in the list for the benefit of future researchers who may attempt to find them.

> ** Wright's first book, *The Fourth Dimension,* has proven impossible to find, though it is mentioned by Wright on a number of occasions and repeatedly listed as one of his publications in his *Who's Who* entry from 1911 until his death in 1949. One can

speculate that this study was an engagement with Charles Howard Hinton's once influential book, also entitled *The Fourth Dimension*, which was published in 1904 and republished in 1906.

EARLY ARTICLES–PRIOR TO BECOMING A FREEMASON (1907–1913)

Prior to becoming a Freemason in 1913, Dudley Wright published articles in a variety of religious, spiritual and esoteric magazines and newspapers, including the Adyar Bulletin, the Annals of Psychical Science, the Bible Review, the Buddhist Review, the Christian Commonwealth, the Homiletic Review, the Mystic, Spiritual Power, and the Theosophist.

ADYAR BULLETIN

The Adyar Bulletin (Journal of the Non-Organized Countries) ran from January 1908 to October 1929, and was published by the Theosophical Publishing House, Adyar, Madras, India. It was founded and edited by Annie Besant. A searchable index can be found at http://www.austheos.org.au/indices/ADYPA1.HTM

Peter, James and John. "Faith, Hope and Love." *Adyar Bulletin*, vol. 4 (February 1911): 37.

"The Effect of Prayer upon Character." *Adyar Bulletin*, vol. 4 (June 1911): 169.

ANNALS OF PSYCHICAL SCIENCE

Wright was Assistant Editor of the annals from circa 1907to 1909 and Editor from October 1909 until the closure in September 1910. According to Wright, the purpose of this periodical was to report "serious and well-attested observations relative to the various psychical phenomena known and studied under the terms Telepathy, Clairvoyance, Premonition, and objective Apparitions."

More Professional "Thought-Readers." *Annals of Psychical Science* 7, no. 47 (November 1908).

BIBLE REVIEW

"The Kingdom of God: What is it?" *Bible Review,* (October 1908).

BUDDHIST REVIEW

The Journal of the Buddhist Society of Great Britain and Ireland. Dudley Wright was briefly the editor of this periodical from circa 1913 to 1914. According to entries in the Buddhist Review, Wright also presented some of the lectures for a course delivered by the Buddhist Society of Great Britain and Ireland.

"Buddhism and Woman." *Buddhist Review,* vol. 3 (1911).

"The Origin and Influence of Buddhism." *Buddhist Review* 5, (July–September 1913).

CHRISTIAN COMMONWEALTH

According to Maurice Canney's *An Encyclopedia of Religions* (1921), the *Christian Commonwealth* was "the originator" of "what was known as the Christian Unity Movement. It persistently attacked the evils of sectarianism and denominationalism. For four or five years it enjoyed the exclusive rights for the weekly serial publications of the sermons of Dr Joseph Parker of the City Temple."

"The Higher Thought Centre." *Christian Commonwealth,* (30 October 1907).

"Christian Science: Two Visits to Sloane Street." *Christian Commonwealth,* (6 November 1907).

"Spiritualism: Interview and Two Séances." *Christian Commonwealth,* (20 November 1907).

"Buddhism in London." *Christian Commonwealth,* (27 November 1907).

"Modern Zoroastrians: Kosmon Church in London." *Christian Commonwealth,* (4 December 1907).

"Students of New Life: Practical Application of Thought." *Christian Commonwealth,* (11 December 1907).

"The Bahai Movement: A Universal Religion." *Christian Commonwealth,* (18

December 1907).

"The New Church: Swedenborgianism." *Christian Commonwealth,* (29 January 1908).

"The Spiritual Mission: Christian Spiritualism." *Christian Commonwealth,* (12 February 1908).

HOMILETIC REVIEW

"Pre-Adamic Man and the Scriptures." *Homiletic Review,* (June 1908).

MYSTIC

Untitled article about Christian Science, originally printed in the *Mystic,* reprinted in *Christian Science Sentinel* (11 July 1908).

SPIRITUAL POWER

Spiritual Power was the journal of the 'Society of the Students of New Life'. It was founded in January 1908 by Samuel George with the help of Dudley Wright. From January to June 1908, Dudley Wright collaborated with Samuel George, the owner of Power-Book, to produce this magazine. They parted company in July 1908.

"Genesis." *Spiritual Power,* (January–April 1908).

"Peter, James and John: Faith, Hope and Love." *Spiritual Power,* (January 1908).

"John I." *Spiritual Power,* (April 1908).

"John II." *Spiritual Power,* (May 1908).

THEOSOPHIST

The Theosophist was founded and edited by Helena Blavatsky in 1879. It was published by the Theosophical Society, Bombay, India. A searchable index can be found at http://www.austheos.org.au/indices/theost.htm

"The Virgin Birth." *The Theosophist,* vol. 32 (November 1910): 215.

"The Prodigal Son." *The Theosophist*, vol. 32 (March 1911): 927.

ARTICLES FOR NON-MASONIC PERIODICALS WHILST A FREEMASON (1913–1932)

Whilst a Freemason, Dudley Wright wrote a number of articles on a variety of religious, spiritual and esoteric subjects for various non-Masonic magazines and newspapers, including the *English Review*, the *Jewish Chronicle*, the *Jewish Guardian*, *Living Age*, the *Occult Review*, and the *Open Court*.

ENGLISH REVIEW

"Charles Lamb and George Dyer." *English Review* (September 1924).

ISLAMIC REVIEW (1915–1920)

Dudley Wright contributed to this magazine during two phases in his life as a Muslim. He embraced Ahmadiyya Islam in 1915 but seemed to drift away from it around 1920. He returned to the Ahmadiyya movement after his Catholic phase at some points in the early 1940s. This section only lists his publications in the *Islamic Review* during his first Islamic phase. His articles published in the *Islamic Review* during the second phase can be found towards the end of this bibliography. *The Islamic Review* (1913–to date) was published by the Woking Muslim Mission which itself was associated with the Shah Jehan Mosque at Woking. It is part of the Ahmadiyya Movement, a moderate branch of Islam, and as such is not always viewed kindly by other parts of the faith. The journal can be viewed online at www.wokingmuslim. org. Originally all articles were published in Woking but by the 1940s printing had been transferred to Lahore.

"The Naturalness of Religion." *Islamic Review*, (September 1915). Extended and reprinted in July-August 1919.

"The Spiritual Basis of Islam." *Islamic Review*, (August 1915). Reprinted in Islamic Review September 1919.

"The Islamic Conception of Deity." *Islamic Review*, (May 1916).

"Characteristics of True Religion." *Islamic Review*, (June 1916). Reprinted in

July–August 1919.

"Islam and Idolatry." *Islamic Review*, (July 1916). Reprinted in September 1919 under the name Muhammad Sadiq Dudley Wright.

"The London Muslim House Sermons: The Essence and Mission of Religion." *Islamic Review*, (January 1919).

"The London Muslim House Sermons: Islamism not Fatalism." *Islamic Review*, (February 1919). This article was published under the name Mohammad Sadiq Dudley Wright. It is the first instance of his using this pen name. In the 1940s he would use it to sign all of his articles in the *Islamic Review*.

"The Practical Duties of Islam." *Islamic Review*, (May 1919).

"Islam: The Faith of Progress." *Islamic Review*, (June 1919).

"The Character of Muhammad." *Islamic Review*, (February 1920).

"The Origin and Development of Sacrifice." *Islamic Review*, (June–July 1920, August–September 1920, and December 1920). The article was published in three instalments; the first under the name D M Sadiq and the latter two under the name Dudley Wright.

Jewish Chronicle and Jewish Guardian

Since its formation in 1841, the *Jewish Chronicle* has been the main weekly communal newspaper for Anglo-Jewry. It has provided a comprehensive picture of Jewish life in England, reported international events of interest to the community, and during the early twentieth century, it printed the minutes of important Jewish institutions such as the Board of Deputies and the Anglo-Jewish Association. Its main rival from 1919 to 1931 was the *Jewish Guardian*. The *Jewish Guardian* did not have the same success as the *Jewish Chronicle* in establishing itself as part of the fabric of the Anglo-Jewish community, and folded in 1931.

"Jews and Freemasonry." *Jewish Guardian*, (5 October 1923).

"Jews as Masonic Leaders." *Jewish Guardian*, (10 October 1924).

"Freemasonry." *Jewish Chronicle*, (2 October 1925).

"Some Notes on the Jews in Oxford." *Jewish Chronicle Supplement*, (October

1929).

"The Book of Raziel." *Jewish Chronicle Supplement,* (October 1931).

"Some Famous Jewish Proselytes." *Jewish Chronicle Supplement,* (October 1933).

LIVING AGE

"Charles Lamb and George Dyer." *Living Age* 36, (4 October 1924).

THE OCCULT REVIEW

Wright published two articles in the *Occult Review* during his early pre-Masonic years, and then four more in the periodical subsequent to 1913. This periodical was a "Monthly Magazine Devoted to the Investigation of Super-Normal Phenomena and the Study of Psychological Problems". Its motto was "Nullius addictus jurare in verba magistri". It was published by William Rider & Son, London. There is an *Occult Review* Index to be found at www.austheos.org.au/indices/occrev.htm

"A Living Vampire." *Occult Review* 12, no.1 (July 1910): 45–48.

"Can Reincarnation be Demonstrated?" *Occult Review* 12, no.4 (October 1910): 221–227.

"Baptism as an Initiatory Rite." *Occult Review* 20, no. 3 (September 1914): 160–162.

"Druidism and Magic." *Occult Review* 21, no. 4 (April 1915): 217–222.

"Druidism–Initiatory Rites–Priesthood." *Occult Review* 24, no. 3 (September 1916): 156–162.

"An Occult Islamic Order." *Occult Review* 38, (December 1923): 365–368.

The *Occult Review* also contained a number of reviews of his various books:

"Review: The Epworth Phenomena by The Editor." *Occult Review* 27, (January 1918): 1.

"Review: The Eleusinian Mysteries and Rites by AE Waite." *Occult Review* 32,

(July 1920): 61.

"Review: Masonic Legends and Traditions by AE Waite." *Occult Review* 34, (September 1921): 186.

"Review: Woman and Freemasonry by EMM." *Occult Review* 35, (June 1922): 319.

THE OPEN COURT

Another periodical that Dudley Wright published an article in during the early years ("Judas and the Kingdom" in 1909) was the *Open Court*. He later returned to the periodical, publishing a dozen articles in its pages from 1918 to 1925. The *Open Court* described itself as being "devoted to the Science of Religion, the Religion of Science, and the Extension of the Religious Parliament Idea." The Open Court Publishing Company was founded in 1887 in LaSalle, Illinois, by Edward Hegeler. Dr Paul Carus, a German-American author with a particular interest in comparative religion, theology, and philosophy, was the magazine's original chief editor. Like Dudley Wright, he was a prolific author, with over 70 books and well over 1000 articles to his credit. An index to Open Court is maintained by the Southern Illinois University and can be viewed at opensiuc.lib.siu.edu/ocj

"Judas and the Kingdom." *The Open Court*, (June 1909): 375–379.

"Druidism." *The Open Court*, (November 1918): 678–684.

"The Affinity of Druidism with Other Religions." *The Open Court*, (March 1921): 129–140.

"Islamic Influence on Jesuit Origins." *The Open Court*, (September 1922): 522–531.

"Some Famous Jewish Proselytes." *The Open Court*, (May 1923): 284–295.

"The Mysteries of the Merkabah." *The Open Court*, (July 1923): 402–407.

"The Religious Opinions of Charles Lamb." *The Open Court*, (November 1923): 641–647.

"Coleridge, Opium and Theology." *The Open Court*, (January 1924): 37–45.

"The Secret Cults of Islam." *The Open Court*, (July 1924): 432–437.

"Gerald Massey." *The Open Court*, (August 1924): 449–457.

"The Burnings of the Talmud." *The Open Court*, (April 1925): 193–217.

ARTICLES FOR MASONIC NEWSPAPERS AND PERIODICALS (1913–1932)

Wright edited and published articles on a variety of Masonic periodicals including the *Masonic Secretaries' Journal*, the *Freemason*, the *Builder*, the *Master Mason*, and the *Masonic News*. He also had a number of articles published in the *British Masonic Miscellany*.

Treasury of Masonic Thought (1924)

A single volume edited by George M Martin & John W Callaghan published in Dundee with one article by Wright.

"Why are we Freemasons?" Dundee, 24–26.

British Masonic Miscellany (1932)

This series was published by George M Martin of Dundee. An examination of the printer's ledgers indicates the whole series were published during 1932. It was an attempt to salvage the Masonic Temple at 31 South Tay St, Dundee, personally run by Bro Martin, from financial ruin. Writers were invited to offer articles which Martin then collated into a series of 20 small volumes of around 150 pages each. This effort failed and the building was turned into a "Palais de Dance".

"Sir Walter Scott and Freemasonry." Vol. 14: 106–118.

"The Eglintons and Mother Kilwinning." Vol. 16: 140–144. It was reprinted from *The Master Mason* (August 1925).

"The Boswells and the Craft." Vol. 17: 118–125. It was reprinted from *The Master Mason* (February 1926).

"The Donoughmores and the Craft." Vol. 17: 134–137.

MASONIC SECRETARIES' JOURNAL

The periodical of the Fratres Calami Lodge (a lodge for the secretaries of other Masonic lodges). The lodge was consecrated in 1917 and their journal only ran until 1919, and then stopped.

1917

"The Future of Freemasonry." *Masonic Secretaries' Journal*, no.2 (September 1917).

1918

"Legends of Solomon, the King." *Masonic Secretaries' Journal*, no.3 (January 1918).

"More Masonic Legends." *Masonic Secretaries' Journal*, no.4 (May 1918).

"Ye Knights of Ye Round Table." *Masonic Secretaries' Journal*, no.5 (September 1918).

1919

"More Masonic Legends." *Masonic Secretaries' Journal*, no.6 (January 1919).

"Our Contributors." *Masonic Secretaries' Journal*, no.6 (January 1919). This is in effect an autobiographical piece by Dudley Wright.

"The Temple in Legend and Tradition." *Masonic Secretaries' Journal*, no.7 (May 1919).

THE FREEMASON

"A Weekly Record of Progress in Freemasonry"

Note: On his departure from *The Freemason* in December 1927, he states that the he has worked at *The Freemason* in various capacities for 16 years. This means a close match between financial troubles at the *London Standard* and his starting at the *Freemason*.

With the exception of "The Future of Freemasonry" in The *Masonic Secre-*

taries' Journal in September 1917, there were no articles on freemasonry by Wright prior to 1918. It seems highly likely that his early function was in the editorial room getting the weekly magazine produced. Whether at *The Freemason* or *The Builder,* his earliest masonic articles start in the second half of 1918. His early contributions relate to ancient mystery orders and are clearly a carryover from past interests and it is almost the end of 1920 before he starts writing typical masonic articles on more traditional subjects.

Those looking at this list need to remember that much of the copies of *The Freemason* were recitation of Lodge and Grand Lodge activities and that the summer break of (typically) June to August meant that a weekly magazine required other materials—usually of a historical nature to fill the gap.

If one counts each part of a multi-issue article individually, then the bibliography runs to approximately 175 articles.

1918

"The Knights of the Round Table." *The Freemason,* (3 August 1918).

"Druidism." *The Freemason,* (17 & 24 August 1918). Published in two instalments.

"Christmas in Pre-Christian Times." *The Freemason,* (14 December 1918).

1919

"The Eleusinian Mysteries and Rites." *The Freemason,* (4 January–3 May 1919). A large essay published in 17 weekly instalments (later republished as a book).

"The Creed of Druidism." *The Freemason,* (24 May–28 June 1919). An article published in 5 weekly instalments.

1920

"Masonic Legends and Traditions." *The Freemason,* (3 January–31 July 1920). A large essay published in 30 weekly instalments (later republished as a book).

"Masonic Legends and Traditions." *The Freemason,* (17 July 1920).

"The Book of Raziel: A Scarce Jewish Work." *The Freemason*, (21 August 1920).

"The Knight and the Mason." *The Freemason*, (23 October 1920).

"First Recorded Initiation in England." *The Freemason*, (6–13 November 1920). An article published in two instalments.

"Secret Societies in the Roman Church." *The Freemason*, (27 November–4 December 1920). An article published in 2 instalments.

"Roman Catholicism & Freemasonry." *The Freemason*, (8 January–1 October 1921). A large essay published in 39 weekly instalments (later republished as a book).

1921

"A Pre-Christian Masonic Philosopher." *The Freemason*, (15 October 1921).

"The Rawlinson Masonic MSS." *The Freemason*, (12 November–26 November 1921). An article published in 3 instalments.

"The Compiler of the Constitutions." *The Freemason*, (7 January 1922).

"The First Grand Chaplain." *The Freemason*, (14 January–21 January 1922). An article published in 2 instalments.

1922

"Freemasonry and the Essenes." *The Freemason*, (4 February–26 August 1922). A large essay published in 29 weekly instalments (most weeks but with some gaps). According to a note in *The Freemason*, it was intended for publication as a book (but it seems this project was never realized).

1923

"Was St. Paulinus a Freemason?" *The Freemason*, (8 September 1923).

"Secret Societies in American Colleges." *The Freemason*, (27 October 1923).

1924

"To Lovers of Charles Lamb." *The Freemason*, (4 October 1924).

1925

"Swedenborg and the Swedenborg Rite." *The Freemason*, (12 September 1925).

1926

"A Priestly Champion of the Craft." *The Freemason*, (21 August 1926).

"Robert Burns & His Publishers." *The Freemason*, (4 September 1926).

"A Noted Masonic Editor of the Past: Bro. the Rev. A. F. A. Woodford, Grand Chaplain, 1864." *The Freemason*, (25 September 1926).

1927

"Burns and his Masonic Circle." *The Freemason*, (28 May–11 June 1927). An article published in 2 instalments.

"Mozart and His Masonic Circle." *The Freemason*, (30 July 1927, 6 August 1927, and 13 August 1927): 117–118. An article in 3 instalments along with a letter.

"Diploma of the Kadriya," *The Freemason*, (20 August 1927): 132.

"The Truth about Daniel O'Connell." *The Freemason*, (20 August 1927): 138–139.

"The Wellesleys and Freemasonry." *The Freemason*, (27 August 1927): 148–149.

"Brother Robert Burns, Jun." *The Freemason*, (3 September 1927): 170.

"The Boswells and the Craft." *The Freemason*, (10 September 1927): 179–180.

"A Priestly Champion of Freemasonry." *The Freemason*, (17 September 1927). Note: the priestly champion was Antione Francois Prevost, d.1763.

"Alexander Gordon: When and Where was he Grand Master." *The Freemason,* (24 September 1927): 211–212.

"Personal." *The Freemason,* (17 December 1927). Announcement by Dudley Wright that he is leaving The Freemason. Management reply on the 24 December 1927.

"William Finch: A Famous Impostor." *The Freemason,* (31 December 1927): 491–492.

THE BUILDER

Copies of the text of all issues of *The Builder* can be found at http://www.phoenixmasonry.org

1918

"Masonic War Work in England." *The Builder,* November 1918. Note: In the article Wright states that he is the Assistant Editor of *The Freemason.*

Significantly, in his regular monthly article, 'An Ambassador', Joseph Fort Newton writes in the March 1918 issue:

> "It is interesting to learn from an article on "Freemasonry in 1917," in the London Times, written by its Masonic editor—Brother Dudley Wright—that the Craft has actually made greater strides during the three years and a half of war than during the same period before the war broke out. Indeed the rush of candidates to its ranks has been so great during the last year that the Grand Lodge of England deemed it wise to limit the number of candidates who could be admitted to any degree at one time to two, instead of five, as was previously the case. This has been so not only in England, but in all Grand Jurisdictions in all lands, except in enemy lands, and of conditions there we have little knowledge."

This is probably the first explicit mention of Wright actually performing the function of "the Masonic Editor". We do not know if that was his official title because all normal articles in *The Times* were without any by-line.

1919

"The Craft in England in 1918, Pt. I," *The Builder*, (February 1919).

"The Eleusinian Mysteries and Rites." *The Builder*, (June–September 1919). An article published in four instalments.

"The Legendary Origin of Freemasonry." *The Builder*, (November 1919).

"Dr George Oliver." *The Builder*, (December 1919).

1920

"The Man Who Saved Burns to Scotland (ed. Thomas Blacklock)," *The Builder*, (July 1920).

"Woman and Freemasonry." *The Builder*, (August 1920).

"Numbers versus Quality." *The Builder*, (September 1920).

"The Hungarian Masonic Persecutions." *The Builder*, (October 1920).

"Woman and Freemasonry." *The Builder*, (October 1920).

"The Knights of Rhodes," *The Builder*, (November 1920). A letter to The Builder.

"Woman and Freemasonry." *The Builder*, (November 1920).

1921

"The Craft in the British Isles in 1920." *The Builder*, (April 1921).

"Secret Societies in the Roman Catholic Church." *The Builder*, (April 1921).

"Roman Catholicism and Freemasonry." *The Builder*, (May–December 1921). An article published in 8 instalments.

"Elias Ashmole and the Masonic Craft." *The Builder*, (June 1921).

"The First Recorded Initiation in England." *The Builder*, (July 1921).

"Masonic Prayers." *The Builder*, (July 1921). A letter to *The Builder*.

"Review of 'Robert Burns and Freemasonry' by Anon." *The Builder,* (August 1921).

"The Roman Catholic Articles." (A response). *The Builder,* (November 1921).

1922

"Dr Wm Stukeley FRS." *The Builder,* (February 1922).

"Review of 'Masonic Legends and Traditions' by Anon." *The Builder,* (February 1922).

"Freemasonry in England in 1921." *The Builder,* (March 1922).

"Martin Foulkes, Deputy Grand Master, 1724." *The Builder,* (April 1922).

1923

"Brother Sir Charles Warren PGD Past District Grand Master, Eastern Archipelago." *The Builder,* (January 1923).

"The Secret Societies of China, Pt. I." *The Builder,* (February–March 1923). An article in 2 parts.

"The Year 1922 in English Masonry." *The Builder,* (March 1923).

"The Grand Master of England." *The Builder,* (November 1923).

1924

"A Striking Incident in English Freemasonry." *The Builder,* (February 1924).

"The Interlaced Triangles." *The Builder,* (February 1924).

"John Theophilus Desaguliers." *The Builder,* (March 1924).

"A Lambskin Lecture." *The Builder,* (April 1924).

1925

"Review of Ashmole: Founder of the Ashmolean Museum, Oxford, by Anon, pub. The Freemason 35pp." *The Builder,* (January 1925).

1926

"Masonic Research." (A letter). *The Builder,* (October 1926).

1930

"A New French Masonic Journal." *The Builder,* (March 1930).

Significantly, the latter article states that:

> "We have received the first issue of *Les Annales Maconniques Universalles.* As the title indicates, it is to be devoted especially to the interests of Universal Masonry, or the Universality of Masonry. We gather that, though there is no direct connection, it will serve as a kind of unofficial or freelance supporter of the aims of the International League of Freemasons (Universala Framasona Liga). Among the contents of this first number is an article on British Masonry by Bro. Dudley Wright."

Note: Copies of *Les Annales Maconniques Universalles* have not as yet been located, and thus the referred to Dudley Wright article in the first issue has not been examined.

The Builder also contained the following reviews of books by Dudley Wright:

July 1925
Meekren, R. J. "Review of Druidism: The Ancient Faith of Britain (London: Ed. J. Burrow, 1924)." *The Builder.* R. J. Meekren was the new editor of The Builder.

April 1927
Anonymous. "Review of The Masonic Who's Who (London: A Lewis, 1926)." *The Builder.* This book was edited by Dudley Wright.

September 1929

J. S. E. "Review of Robert Burns and his Masonic Circle (London: Cecil Palmer, 1929)." *The Builder.*

THE MASTER MASON

Published by the Masonic Service Association of the United States (later of North America) at $3 per year. The editorial team was initially Joseph Fort Newton LittD Editor, Andrew L Randall Managing Editor, Roscoe Pound LLD, Dudley Wright, JH Tatsch (Tatsch left as an Editor by September 1924 with Carl Claudy taking his place in October) as Contributing Editors. In 1927 the editorial team changed to be Joseph Fort Newton LittD Editor, Andrew L Randall LLD Managing Editor, Carl H Claudy and Frederick W Hamilton LLD as Associate Editors, together with Roscoe Pound LLD, Henry R Evans LittD, and Dudley Wright as Contributing Editors.

The monthly magazine ran from January 1924 to 1930 and seems to have ceased publication after it left the control of the Masonic Service Association. Copies can be found at the University of Oxford, Biblioteque Nationale de France, Paris and in various US libraries, and masonic libraries. The authors acknowledge the assistance of Larissa Watkins of the House of the Temple Library in Washington DC.

1924

"The Prime Minister of Masonry: Sketch of the Right Worshipful Brother Sir Alfred Robbins." *The Master Mason* 1, no. 1 (January 1924): 38–46.

"Bro Lord Ampthill: Sketch of the Pro Grand Master of England." *The Master Mason* 1, no. 5 (May 1924): 314–317.

"The Home of English Masonry." *The Master Mason* 1, no. 9 (September 1924): 383–385.

"The Mark Degree." *The Master Mason* 1, no. 10 (October 1924): 637–639.

"Brother Rudyard Kipling." *The Master Mason* 1, no. 11 (November 1924): 659–660.

"Alexander Gordon." *The Master Mason* 1, no. 12 (December 1924): 841–845.

"Martin Faulks' Cocked Hat." *The Master Mason* 1, no. 12 (December 1924): 850–851.

1925

"Brother Sir Charles Cameron." *The Master Mason* 2, no. 1 (January 1925): 53–56.

"An Interesting Masonic Record." *The Master Mason* 2, no. 2 (February 1925): 97–100.

"Wellesleys and Freemasonry." *The Master Mason* 2, no. 3 (March 1925): 187–190.

"A Famous Masonic Litteratuer." *The Master Mason* 2, no. 4 (April 1925): 312–313.

"Burns Robert Sr, Robert Jr and Gilbert." *The Master Mason* 2, no. 5 (May 1925): 385–393.

"Some Curious Initiations." *The Master Mason* 2, no. 6 (June 1925): 477–486.

"The Eglintons & Mother Kilwinning." *The Master Mason* 2, no. 8 (August 1925): 645–648.

"Orator John Henley: An Eccentric Grand Chaplain." *The Master Mason* 2, no. 9 (September 1925): 764–766.

"Two Masonic Friends of Robert Burns." *The Master Mason* 2, no. 11 (November 1925): 932–936.

1926

"Why are we Apprentices?" *The Master Mason* 3, no. 1 (January 1926): 62–64.

"The Boswells and the Craft." *The Master Mason* 3, no. 2 (February 1926): 147–150.

"Freemasonry in England in 1925." *The Master Mason* 3, no. 3 (March 1926): 219–221.

"The Ante Room: The Masonic career of Robert Burns." *The Master Mason* 3, no. 5 (May 1926): 451–454.

"The Ante Room: Freemasonry in Jamaica." *The Master Mason* 3, no.7 (July 1926): 653–656.

"The Ante Room: A Celebrated Masonic Character." *The Master Mason* 3, no. 9 (September 1926): 821–822.

"English Freemasonry before the Era of Grand Lodges Robert Freke Gould." *The Master Mason.* (anon but surely via DW).

"Freemasonry in the British Isles Anon." *The Master Mason,* (October 1926): 878–879. (probably by Wright)

"The Ante Room: An Initiation with a Mystery." *The Master Mason* 3, no. 10 (October 1926): 912–913.

1927

"Preston and the Prestonian Lecture." *The Master Mason* 4, no. 5 (May 1927): 355–357.

"The Lodge of the Nine Muses." *The Master Mason* 4, no. 6 (June 1927): 459–462.

"The Ante Room." *The Master Mason* 4, no. 9 (September 1927): 703–709.

"The Royal Order of Scotland." *The Master Mason* 4, no. 10 (October 1927): 773–776.

"The Swedenborg Rite." *The Master Mason* 4, no. 11 (November 1927): 861–863.

1928

"The Ancient and Primitive Rite." *The Master Mason* 5, no. 1 (January 1928): 41–44.

"The Ante Room: Royal Masonic Benevolent Institution." *The Master Mason* 5, no. 2 (February 1928): 133–135.

"England's Royal Family and The Craft." *The Master Mason* 5, no. 7 (July 1928): 432–438.

"Eustace Blugdell Freemason." *The Master Mason* 5, no. 10 (October 1928): 699–701.

1929

"Patrick Bramwell Bronte." *The Master Mason* 6, no.1 (January 1929): 32–34.

"The Ante Room: Freemasonry in Cambridge, England." *The Master Mason* 6, no. 3 (March 1929): 206–208.

"The Ante Room: Freemasonry in England since the Armistice." *The Master Mason* 6, no. 4 (April 1929): 278.

"The Ante Room: Gateshead Lodge of Industry." *The Master Mason* 6, no. 5 (May 1929): 350–352.

"The Ancient and Primitive Rite." *The Master Mason* 6, no. 10 (October 1929): 663–667.

1930

No articles by Dudley Wright in this year. Note: the final issue held in the library at the House of the Temple, and apparently the final issue of the periodical, was dated March–April 1930.

MASONIC NEWS (1928–1931)

There are 8 bound volumes in the Library and Museum of Freemasonry in London. The final one, volume 8, only contains a few issues in July 1931. Four volumes containing this newspaper can also be found at the British Library. Because the coverage was mostly on lodge and Grand Lodge events, there was a shortage of copy during the summer recess months and usually considerably more educational content. There are odd bits on Chapters but nothing really on other orders. Like *The Freemason,* it is full of centenaries and installations, together with the usual Grand Lodge charity and masonic hospital material.

Volume 1

"A Famous Lodge (ed. Apollo Lodge, Oxford)." *Masonic News* 1, no. 12 (24 March 1928): 228.

"Peter Sthael: Rosicrucian." *Masonic News* 1, no. 12 (24 March 1928): 240

"Freemasonry in Finland." *Masonic News* 1, no. 13 (31 March 1928): 261.

"Early German Freemasonry." *Masonic News* 1, no. 13 (31 March 1928): 257–258.

"Early Freemasonry in Oxford." *Masonic News* 1, no. 14 (1928): 286–288.

"Jews and Freemasonry." *Masonic News* 1, no. 16 (1928): 306–307.

"English Speaking Grand Lodges and the French Grand Orient." *Masonic News* 1, no. 17 (1928).

"The First Papal Masonic Bull." *Masonic News* 1, no. 18 (1928): 367–368.

"Bro Abdeali Shaik Mahomedali Anik." *Masonic News* 1, (2 June 1928): 440.

Volume 2

"The Secret Cults of Islam." *Masonic News* 2, no. 29 (21 July1928): 57–58.

"The Quakers and the Craft." *Masonic News* 2, no. 31 (1928): 84.

"Freemasonry in Bohemia." *Masonic News* 2, (1928): 103–104.

"The Largest Pyramid in the World." *Masonic News* 2, no. 33 (1928): 119–120.

"Masonic Research." *Masonic News* 2, no. 34 (25 August 1928): 132.

"Freemasonry in the Law Courts." *Masonic News* 2, no. 34 (25 August 1928) 135–136.

"Masons and Catholics." *Masonic News* 3, (27 October 1928): 320. It was originally printed in the Catholic newspaper, The Universe, on 19 October 1928.

"The Order of the Kadriya." *Masonic News* 3, no. 65 (23 March 1929): 226–227.

"Freemasonry in Cambridge." *Masonic News* 3, no. 67 (6 April 1929): 263–264.

"Freemasonry in Iowa." *Masonic News* 3, no. 67 (6 April 1929): 278.

Volume 4

"The Book of Raziel: A Scarce Jewish Work." *Masonic News* 4, no. 82 (27 July 1929): 76.

"Mount Carmel." *Masonic News* 4, no. 82 (3 August 1929): 88–89. Reprinted with permission from the *New Age Magazine,* the organ of the AASR (SJ).

"(Roman) Catholicism and Freemasonry." *Masonic News* 4, no. 84 (1929): 112–113.

"The Gateshead Lodge of Industry." *Masonic News* 4, no. 86 (24 August 1929): 146–147.

"William Preston, Eminent Masonic Scholar." *Masonic News* 4, no. 87 (31 August 1929). (Copyright Masonic Service Association of the United States, reprinted by permission). Need to check text.

"The International League of Freemasons." *Masonic News* 4, no. 90 (21 September 1929): 226–227. Dudley Wright's record of his attendance at the 4th congress in Amsterdam (Thursday, 12 September to Sunday 15 September 1929).

"Mount Hermon." *Masonic News* 4, no. 101 (7 Dec 1929).

"A Masonic Dream." *Masonic News* 4, no. 103 (21 Dec 1929): 495–496. This article has no stated author, but in it the unspecified author states that he dreamed that all those who had not paid him for their subscriptions, some of them for 2 years were going to do so. Clearly money was already an issue after only 24 months. The style of writing was that of Dudley Wright, and he was almost certainly its anonymous author.

Volume 5

"Initiation among the Essenes." *Masonic News* 5, (4 January 1930): 7–9.

"The Mysteries of the Merkabah." *Masonic News* 5, (11 January 1930): 43–35.

"Review of A R Robbins book English Speaking Freemasonry." *Masonic News* 5, (26 April 1930): 339. While not named, the author is almost certainly Wright.

Volume 6

"The Egyptian Society." *Masonic News* 6, no. 131 (5 July 1930): 3–4.

"Freemasonry in Germany." *Masonic News* 6, no. 134 (19 July 1930). Unnamed, but probably Wright.

"The Eglintons and Mother Killwinning." *Masonic News* 6, no. 135 (2 August 1930): 71–72.

"The Wellesley and Freemasonry." *Masonic News* 6, no. 136 (9 August 1930): 96–97.

"A Famous Scottish Judge and Grand Warden (Lord Elgin)." *Masonic News*6. No. 138 (2 August 1930): 126.

Volume 7

There were no articles by Wright in this volume.

Volume 8

Volume 8 only contains issues for July 1931. These were thin issues and short of content. The final issue in the volume was dated 18 July 1931. There were no obvious pieces authored by Dudley Wright in these final issues or, indeed, from August 1930 onwards. Furthermore, with the exception of one article in the *Jewish Chronicle* in October 1931, it seems that he published no articles in any journal during this year. Presumably, the pressure of keeping the business going was having an impact on his opportunities for writing.

CATHOLIC PERIODICALS (1932–1938)

Wright embraced Catholicism at some point towards the end of 1932 or the beginning of 1933 (no exact date available). He became a member of the Catholic Guild of Israel on 28 October 1933 (the date can be found in the membership book of the Catholic Guild of Israel, held in the Guild's archives, which are currently looked after by the Sisters of Sion in London—see the final section of this bibliography). Wright published articles in the *New Black-friars* (the periodical of the British Dominicans), *Our Lady of Sion* (the periodical of the Catholic Guild of Israel), and the *Catholic Herald*. Around this time, he also had letters published in other Catholic newspapers such as the *Catholic Times* and the *Tablet*.

"Freemasonry in Spain since 1728, Letter to the Editor." *Catholic Times* (23 September 1932).

"Freemasonry in Spain, Letter to the Editor." *Catholic Times* (21 October 1932).

"Communism in the British Museum, Letter to the Editor." *Catholic Times* (28 October 1932).

"Charles Lamb and St. Thomas Aquinas." *New Blackfriars* 14, no. 155 (February 1933).

"Some Papal Edicts Against Judaism." *Our Lady of Sion* 41, (Spring 1934).

"Psychical Phenomena (a review of "Psychical Phenomena of Jamaica" by Joseph J. Williams)." *The Catholic Herald* (9 February 1935).

"The Blood Accusation Libel." *Our Lady of Sion* 53, (Spring 1938).

"From Rabbi to Archbishop." *Our Lady of Sion* 53, (Summer 1938).

ISLAMIC REVIEW (1944–1949)

For his earlier articles in the *Islamic Review,* and a brief description of the periodical, see the section on articles for non-Masonic periodicals whilst a Freemason (towards the beginning of this bibliography).

The following articles were published under the name Muhammad Sadiq Dudley Wright:

"The Futility of Christian Missions." *Islamic Review,* (June 1944).

"The Uniqueness of Islam." *Islamic Review,* (November 1944).

"The Missions of Jesus and Muhammad." *Islamic Review,* (February 1945).

"Muslims Arise! A Call to Action!" *Islamic Review,* (May 1946)

"The Decline of Christianity." *Islamic Review,* (June 1946)

"The Five Pillars of Islam." *Islamic Review,* (July-August 1946).

"Desperate Christians." *Islamic Review,* (September 1946).

"The Changing Church." *Islamic Review,* (December 1946).

"Islam and Climatology." *Islamic Review,* (February 1947).

"Five Pillars of Islam." *Islamic Review,* (March 1947).

"Five Pillars of Islam – The Fourth Pillar." *Islamic Review,* (April–May 1947).

"IF." *Islamic Review,* (July 1947)

"Five Pillars of Islam – The Fifth Pillar." *Islamic Review,* (August 1947).

"Does Christianity Need More Leaven?" *Islamic Review,* (September 1947).

"The Parable of the Prodigal." *Islamic Review,* (November 1947).

"Prophethood in Judaism and Islam." *Islamic Review,* (December 1947).

"Is One Religion As Good As Another?" *Islamic Review,* (January 1948).

"Fourscore Years: Retrospect." *Islamic Review,* (February 1948).

"Truth in Controversy." *Islamic Review,* (March 1948).

"Additional Notes on the First Pillar." *Islamic Review,* (June 1948).

"Who Were the Essenes? Was Jesus an Essene?" *Islamic Review,* (July 1948).

"Who Were the Essenes? Was Jesus an Essene?" *Islamic Review,* (August–September 1948).

UNPUBLISHED MANUSCRIPTS –
CATHOLIC GUILD OF ISRAEL

"The Spanish Inquisition and the Jews" (unpublished manuscript). Circa, 1934.

"St. Gregory the Great" (unpublished manuscript). Circa, 1934.

The two unpublished manuscripts, 3 letters to Sister Mary Pancratius (dated 12 February 1934; 8 March 1934; 23 February 1935), and the Catholic Guild of Israel Membership Book containing an entry for Dudley Wright (dated 28 October 1933), are all held in the archives of the Catholic Guild of Israel. The Catholic Guild of Israel ceased to exist sometime around 1940 (no exact date), but its "archives" are now held by the Sisters of Sion at the following address: Sion Centre for Dialogue and Encounter, 34 Chepstow Villas, London, W11 2QZ. The archives of the Guild consist of 9 boxes.

THE TIMES, LONDON

While Wright claimed in *The Builder* to be the Masonic Editor of *The Times* of London, it was in a recent study by Dr Paul Calderwood that the extent of this was discovered. Wright published about 815 short articles relating to Freemasonry in *The Times* newspaper from 1919 until 1933. It was computed by Calderwood from the detailed records left by the clerks of the newspaper's accounting department whose detailed records of every payment remained in the archives.

E&OE.

It used to be common to see at the bottom of invoices the letters E&OE, meaning "Errors and Omissions Excepted". In delving among numerous records to construct this bibliography, we have repeatedly found that there is more to be discovered. We have not searched either the United States masonic journals or anything in South Africa or Australia. There will be more, but increasingly it is likely to be reprints of existing listed materials rather than unlisted articles. We apologize if there are any serious omissions still to be discovered.

Dudley Wright: Disambiguation

There were several prominent Dudley Wrights at the end of the nineteenth century and during the first half of the twentieth century. These are often returned by search engines and are easily confused. This is illustrated by a number of websites and articles that have mistakenly combined facts and photos relating to different Dudley Wrights. A disambiguation is, thus, helpful between our Dudley Wright (1868–1949) and the others: Dudley d'Auvergne Wright (1867–1948), Dudley Wright Knox (1877–1960), and H. Dudley Wright (c. 1920–January 1992).

1. **The Dudley Wright (1868–1949)** discussed in this book was born in London. By profession he was a writer, concerned initially with "psychical research," spiritualism, the occult, and theosophy, and later with Buddhism, Judaism, Catholicism, and the Ahmadiyya movement within Islam. He was also a Freemason and the majority of his writings were concerned with Freemasonry. He wrote for masonic magazines in both the United Kingdom and United States.

2. **Dudley d'Auvergne Wright (1867–1948)** was born at Colombo, Ceylon (now Sri Lanka). He was initially a traditional physician who later embraced homeopathy, and trained and served as a surgeon at the London Homeopathic Hospital. He was captured and interned in Berlin during World War II, and "repatriated" to South Africa. He later settled and died at Bembridge, Isle of Wight. He wrote extensively on his fields of expertise. See the Royal College of Surgeons entry: http://livesonline.rcseng.ac.uk/biogs/E004817b.htm

3. **Commodore Dudley Wright Knox (1877–1960)** was born in Washington DC and graduated from the United States Naval Academy in 1896. He fought in the Spanish–American War of 1898 and in World War I. He later became a naval historian and published in that field several books concerned with naval history and strategy. For more information, see: https://en.wikipedia.org/wiki/Dudley_Wright_Knox

4. **H. Dudley Wright (c. 1920–January 1992)** was born in America. He was an entrepreneur, self-taught engineer, and inventor. In 1947, he

founded a successful company in Pasadena, California, manufacturing piezo-electric instruments. He moved to Geneva in 1965. The aim of his life was to advocate community and business investment to increase the general public's knowledge of science. He died in Switzerland in 1992. His work continues to this day through the Swiss Foundation H. Dudley Wright. For more information, see: www.hdwright.org

Appendix I

Biographical excerpt from *The Masonic Secretaries' Journal.*

We intend, when time and opportunity allow, to present pen-pictures of our Contributors. The difficulty was with whom to commence. Ultimately our choice fell upon Bro. Dudley Wright, whose works and literary contributions are are known to many of the readers of The Masonic Secretaries' Journal, was for many years a member of the editorial staff of the ill-fated *Standard* newspaper. He is a man of great energy and of many and varied attainments. His journalistic career extends to nearly 30 years, and his aquaintance with Pitman's system of shorthand dates back to to the year 1878. He was born in Cheyne Walk, Chelsea, in 1868, and was thus during his early years a neighbour of Thomas Carlyle. On his mother's side he comes from an old Scottish family. His father was an East Anglian.

Bro. Wright's particular hobby has always been the study of Comparative Religions. His first published work, "The Fourth Dimension," was sold out within three months of publication. His next work, "Was Jesus an Essene?" elicited high commendation from several authorities on the subject, but particularly from the late Bro. Dr. Christian Ginsburg, the well-known Hebraist, himself the author of a work on the Essenes, and the father of Bro. Dr. Benedict Ginsburg, one of the contributors to the present issue of The Masonic Secretaries' Journal. In pursuit of his hobby Bro. Dudley Wright became for a time editor (unpaid) of *The Buddhist Review,* and one of the books which stand to the credit of his pen is the *Manual of Buddhism,* published in 1912 by Messrs. Kegan, Paul & Co., and which bore an introduction by Prof. Edmund Mills, F.R.S., then Chairman of the Council of the Buddhist Society of Great Britain and Ireland. Bro. Dudley Wright's aim has been to trace the unvarying basis from the philosophical standpoint, of all religious systems, an Islamic belief, which has made him a welcome lecturer at the Mosque at Woking, on the Buddhist platform, in Jewish gatherings, and on the platform of Christian societies, and until the outbreak of the war he was a constant lecturer in all parts of England, Scotland and Wales. His frequent magazine contributions have included in their range journals which might be regarded by some as poles asunder, such as the *Homeletic Review,* the *Open Court,* the *Bible Review,* the *Islamic Review,* the *Crescent,* the *Primitive Methodist Review,* the *Theosophist,* the *Theosophical Review,* the *Adyar Bulletin,* the *Occult Review,* the *Harbinger of Light* (Australia), and the *Kalpaka,* and Indian magazine, and our Journal.

One of his best-known books is *Prayer,* published by the Theosophical Publishing Society. Bro. Dudley Wright has never associated himself with the Theosophical movement, but Mrs. Besant, referring to his contributions to literature, described the author as "that clever writer." The shilling book, although published six years ago, is still a "good seller." Another of his works, published since the outbreak of the war, is *Vampires and Vampirism,* an exhaustive treatise of this legend, to which is appended a bibliography of works on the subject, and, more recently, he has published *The Epworth Phenomena and Other Psychic Experiences of John Wesley, personal and narrated.* Among the translations he has published is a standard work in the French language by Dr. Paul Joire, entitled *Physical and Supernormal Phenomena,* and his magazine contributions have included translations from the Swedish, Italian, and Spanish, as well as the French languages.

During the past few years Bro. Dudley Wright has devoted much time to the study of Freemasonry, and there is awaiting publication his work on *Robert Burns and Freemasonry,* which, when it appeared in serial form in the columns of *The Freemason* evoked much praise. Since then the articles have been considerably extended. Another work which Bro. Dudley Wright has completed and which will shortly see the light of day in print is *Woman and Freemasonry.* As subjects closely identified with Masonic origins he has ready for publication an exhaustive treatise on Druidism and another on the Eleusinian Rites, which have been withheld solely by reason of the prevailing conditions in the paper and printing trades. As is well known, Bro. Dudley Wright is the assisstant editor of *The Freemason,* but he is known as a frequent contributor to *The Builder,* an organ of the Masonic Research Association of America; *The Masonic Standard* of New York; *The*

Masonic Journal of South Africa, and last, but by no means least,
THE MASONIC SECRETARIES' JOURNAL.

EDITORIAL NOTE.—We are so constantly being asked questions in refer-
ence to the works of Bro. Dudley Wright, it will be a convenience if members will write direct to Bro. Wright at his private address, 10 Beaumont
Bulidings, Oxford. On request, he promises to send a full list of his published works, the prices of which range from one shilling to about half-a-
guinea.

APPENDIX II

The

Islamic Review

FOUNDED BY THE LATE AL-HAJJ KHWAJA KAMAL-UD-DIN
Editors : M. Abdul Majid, M.A. and M. Aftab-ud-Din Ahmad, B.A.

Vol. XXXVI	RABĪ' AL-THĀNI 1367 A.H.	No.
	FEBRUARY 1948 C.E.	
Annual Subscription 12s. or Rs. 7/8/-		Single Copy 1s.

CONTENTS

		Page
BY THE LIGHT OF THE HOLY QUR-AN	...	41
A DECLARATION	...	42
MAHATMA GANDHI	...	42
FOURSCORE YEARS—RETROSPECT		
By Muhammad Sadiq Dudley Wright, Phil. D., F.S.P. ...		47
THE WAY OF LIFE—The Guidance (6)		
By W. B. Bashyr Pickard, B.A. (Cantab)	...	52
JESUS—SON OF MARY—HIS BIRTH & DEATH		
By Khawaja Nazir Ahmad	...	58
CORRESPONDENCE	...	77
WHAT IS ISLAM?	...	79

Published by :
THE WOKING MUSLIM MISSION AND LITERARY TRUST
THE SHAH JEHAN MOSQUE,
WOKING, SURREY, ENGLAND.

85

FOURSCORE YEARS : RETROSPECT

By MUHAMMAD SADIQ DUDLEY WRIGHT, PHIL. D.,F.S.P.,
MEMBER OF THE HISTORICAL ASSOCIATION.

To one who can take a retrospective view over a longer period than that defined by the psalmist as the span of human life, there is much to cheer and comfort in that view, much also, alas ! to sadden and regret.

Seventy years ago, pessimism, not optimism, was the dominant note in sermons, hymns, prayers and conversation. There were few who believed in the optimism of Robert Browning, fewer still willing to accept his challenge to

> Grow old along with me,
> The best is yet to be,
> The last of life for which
> The first was made,
> The whole is in His hand
> Who said A whole I planned,
> Trust God, see all nor be afraid.

There were fewer still who were willing to accept the dictum of his compeer, Tennyson, that

> There lives more faith in honest doubt,
> Believe me, than in half the creeds.

What was the gospel preached in the majority of churches and chapels of Britain seventy years ago ? Its dominant feature was Calvinism, sometimes aggressively paraded. Self-constituted evangelists haunted the main thoroughfares of cities and towns and intercepted pedestrians, whether walking singly or with friends with impertinent personal questions, such as : "Where will you spend eternity, sister ?" or " Are you saved, brother ?" or "Have you found the Lord, brother ?" One asked this last question of a resident seated one Sunday afternoon on the front at Littlehampton and went away screaming. "Blasphemer !" when he received the reply : "No, good heavens ! have you lost him ?" Since those days, however, sermons have become less aggressive, possibly by reason of the diminution of both evangelists and congregations ; but mainly, I think, because there has been a great revolution in thought. Indeed, the character of the services held in the buildings set apart for preaching and what is termed 'worship' has become radically changed. The cinema has taken the place of the enquiry room and the penitent form. John Calvin no longer pulls the strings.

Great, indeed, also is the alteration that has taken place in the attitude of the religious world towards Science. Darwin, Wallace, Huxley and many others whose names have become household words, are no longer branded as atheists, or even as sceptics : and their science is no longer regarded as atheistic. When it was first pointed out that Darwin's original intention was to be ordained as a clergyman, that neither Wallace nor Huxley was ever an atheist, people began to regard them as backsliders. To-day the bones or ashes of the world's greatest contributors to science lie in that vast hall of Hela, called Westminster Abbey, regardless of the religion or non-religion they professed in life, while man with high scientific attainments, sometimes with negative opinions as regards religion stand in the pulpit, certain of attracting large congregations.

The doctrine of Evolution was first hailed as the product of Atheism. To-day it is welcomed by all the sects as having been taught by Augustine. Some Christian apologists have gone even further and have twisted texts about to demonstrate that it is a scriptural doctrine. When, in 1909, the jubilee of the first publication of the *Origin of Species* was celebrated at Cambridge, there appeared on the platform a Roman Catholic Canon, who afterwards incorporated his contribution in a published volume, designed to demonstrate that it had always been the teaching of the Church of which he was a representative.

To a very great extent belief in an infallible church had been waning for many years when the nineteenth century was marking its closing years. It had been supplanted in a great measure by belief in an infallible Bible, but the wreckage of that belief had also been inaugurated by the unanswerable onslaught of biblical criticism. For a time partial inspiration took its place, but there were none to say what parts were inspired.

FOURSCORE YEARS : RETROSPECT

To-day we are told, as one minister did say :

"Of course the Bible is inspired, just as a treatise on mathematics or science is inspired."

What is the prevailing fad of the Church of England to-day ? It would seem to be ritual, its ministers dressing up in gaudy, theatrical attire, genuflecting and bowing as frequently as possible, studying colour schemes and devising fresh 'aids to devotion.' The early Tractarians were not ritualists. They believed they had a message to deliver and they did deliver the message, which was the continuity of the Church, without the aid or hindrance of special garments. Ritualism was an after-thought. A one-time friend was a priest of the Roman communion, his headquarters or mission being in an unpretentious building in a London slum. He noticed as a regular attender at the services an elderly woman, whom he never saw at Communion. One evening he made the opportunity of speaking to her, and saying he did not remember her name. "Oh, no", she said, "you see, I belong to—" mentioning a well-known Ritualistic church in the vicinity. "Well," said my friend, "we are pleased to see you and hope you will always come here, but why don't you go to your own church ?" "Well," was her reply, "you see they are much too 'high' for me. I like your services better and you are all so homely here."

I once heard Dr. Estlin Carpenter say from the pulpit of Manchester College Chapel at Oxford, towards the close of his long and useful life that he had found the earth a very interesting dwelling-place because of the changes he had witnessed in religious action and thought. Changes in that thought have been so radical and wide-spread that even the exertion put forth recently to brand Bishop Barnes as a heretic resembled the ignition of a dampened squib. But the bishop's attitude was by no means new or novel. Less than a hundred years ago a bishop of the Church of England published freethought tracts through a recognized freethought publisher. His name was Hind and he was for eight years Bishop of Norwich. He was also one of the original committee, along with Sir Charles Lyall and Charles Darwin, formed for the foundation of the Theistic Church in London under the direction of the

Rev. Charles Yoysey, who was deprived of his living at
Healaugh, but was not excommunicated because the
Church of England has no power of excommunication.
The "heresies" as they were called, propounded by
another bishop—Co-lenso—are now generally accepted
as truths. Since then there have been many persecutions
and prosecutions of ritualistic offenders, which we
octogenarians can well remember, when bricks and stones
were hurled at the offenders, some of whom were sent
to prison for their opinions and practices. These
incidents have now passed into history. To-day there
is only one church in London where the black gown is
seen in the pulpit—supposed to be the hall-mark of
evangelism—when the sermon is preached. To-day
churches are being demolished, because, it is said, of
bomb damage, but the fact is they have lost their
usefulness. They have become superfluous. One of
them is situate in the street in which I live. A few days
ago I was discussing the subject with a ritualistic curate
of the adjoining parish and in speaking of the vicar of
the condemned church, he remarked: "Well, he is
going to a very fine church in a nice neighbourhood and
where they have a lovely ritual." Not a word as to
whether he would have increased opportunities for
service, which was a recommendation of Jesus. We are
told only of pleasure at the increased opportunities the
change would give him for 'dressing-up' and for greater
theatrical display.

One great change that has taken place will commend
itself to all thinkers in the attitude of men, whether they
accept the qualifying adjective of 'religious' or not : that
is the attitude towards opponents. The days are past and
gone or, at any rate, fast receding, when religion was the
butt of satire and ridicule, particularly of pictorial
caricature, which, to sober minds, was unseemly. This
changed attitude was ably portrayed by Edna Lyall in her
novel *We Two* and anticipated before her day in many
of the poems by Burns and, of course, by other poets
and prose writers, though his was the greater influence.
The most modern attitude finds expression in the more
sober presentation in what is known as Rationalism.

An even more striking illustration of the change in
thought is the fact that among Rationalist writers and

lecturers are to be found members of the Anglican communion and Nonconformist ministers and the laity of both. Some, like the late Moncure D. Conway, have travelled to the Rationalist view from Methodism and other sects via Unitarianism.

What bearing have these facts upon Islam ? First, I think, it should be encouragement. Not long since I was in correspondence with a well-known Unitarian minister, I was going to describe him as 'highly-educated' but that would be a superficiality because all Unitarians are educated and the ministers, as well as the majority of the laity, highly educated. In some publications he sent me the claims of Unitarianism were ably presented. but I wrote to him and said it was my privilege, which I accounted an honour, to belong to the oldest and largest Unitarian community the world had ever known, *i.e.*, the Faith of Islam, founded centuries before the birth of Socinus, generally accredited to have been the founder of Unitarianism. The development of religious thought and its attitude towards orthodox Christianity, which all Muslims recognize as a departure from the teaching of Jesus, is the recognition of man's duty to God and attitude of service to His creatures. It is a development of the apostolate, not confined to a dozen members or to a select hierarchy, but includes all who are proud to respond to the title of Muslim, who recognize and regard the Holy Prophet Muhammad as the Apostle of God, the messenger of Allah, who seek by their lives to spread the truth among the nations. The task is not an easy one, even in these days of liberal thought : it is as difficult now as it was in the days when the rack and gibbet and stake were at the end of the road along which the apostle had to travel, on which he had to walk with blood-stained feet. The work is hard but yet the labour is sweet, as are the rewards. It has to be pursued in recognition of the demands of Allah, the Lord of All the Worlds. It cannot be done by preaching or talking alone and these even are less effective than living the life. Think of the many irrefragable testimonies towards the power of Islam by non-Islamic writers, who have written of the life of the

"Men of Prayer, whose Mosque is in them everywhere."

Remember, too, the words of the prophet Zacharia'ı towards the Jews :

Thus saith the Lord of Hosts, in those days, ten men shall take hold out of all languages of the nations, even shall take hold of the skirt of him that is a Jew, saying : We will go with you; for we have heard that God is with you.

Living, not oral, preaching is the pleasurable privilege of every Muslim, one calculated; to borrow a phrase from R.W. Trine, to bring the individual "in tune with the Infinite." Simple we may be and the odds against us may be incredible, but highly educated we shall become in the ways of Allah and Victory is assured.

www.ingramcontent.com/pod-product-compliance
Lightning Source LLC
Chambersburg PA
CBHW060512280326
41933CB00014B/2932